Finding Grace in the Moment

Finding Grace in the Moment

✦

Stories and Other Musings of an Aged Monk

Fr. Simeon Daly, OSB

iUniverse, Inc.
New York Lincoln Shanghai

Finding Grace in the Moment
Stories and Other Musings of an Aged Monk

iUniverse books may be ordered through booksellers or by contacting:

iUniverse
2021 Pine Lake Road, Suite 100
Lincoln, NE 68512
www.iuniverse.com
1-800-Authors (1-800-288-4677)

ISBN-13: 978-0-595-35455-9 (pbk)
ISBN-13: 978-0-595-79948-0 (ebk)
ISBN-10: 0-595-35455-6 (pbk)
ISBN-10: 0-595-79948-5 (ebk)

Printed in the United States of America

Contents

Preface

It is not without some angst that I make the following stories and essays available in such a permanent form. It is not a new struggle. I have already been through it before, since about half of them have already been made available on CDs and on an Internet Web site. Many of them are very personal. Practically none of them was written for publication. They have grown out of moments of my life or from my reflections on special moments. However, I have been strongly encouraged by friends to share them even after, or perhaps because, they had listened to my reading of some of them.

I am also encouraged by my own conviction that sharing such stories, especially those that touch on the core values of our lives, evokes in the listener a desire to share his or her own story. Reading a good story can stimulate the reader to comb through personal experiences where similar moments have been had. Perhaps they are in touch with their own stories, but the reflection may awaken a sudden awareness of similar moments of grace. It is with the hope that this will happen that I dare to lay these out.

Over a luncheon with two friends one day in July of 2003, in a moment that I seem to recall was reluctant, I agreed to take steps to see that some of my stories were made public. I had already given the idea some thought, but I promised to look into it. One of the gentlemen, one accustomed to having his way, said he would send a Dictaphone for me to dictate the stories. He would have them transcribed and printed up and he would provide copies to me and to his friends.

Later in the quiet of my cell, I decided against that method, figuring if I were to do it at all I should do it properly, in our studio, with the help of a professional technician. I wrote the gentleman to that effect. Too late, he had already sent the Dictaphone. I ignored it and went about getting permissions and making inquiries about financial and technical support. My efforts seemed to be going nowhere as days passed into weeks. Finally, after staring at that little machine sitting idle on my desk, I decided to go ahead and read some stories onto the hand-held dictation machine right there in my office. Given my age, I could well be incapacitated before anything got moving through the channels I was pursuing.

After I had filled four mini-cassettes with stories, I shipped them off to my friend. At this point, I was more interested in voice recording than print. I had most of the stories in machine-readable form already. It would not be necessary for some secretary to transcribe them. One of the two gentlemen, with professional help, had the stories transposed into audio files and CDs were developed. Later those CDs were reformatted and I had the stories published professionally. That process was underwritten by a few generous donations from family and friends.

The warmth with which those CDs have been received has motivated me to take this next step of putting them in print. If you have read this, I hope you will move on to the stories, and if you read the stories, I sincerely hope you will not be disappointed. Please pray for the author.

Small Beginnings

It was September, I remember, that first time I saw the Abbey towers, September 1936. I quaked a little inside wondering in my timid heart what I was getting myself into. The story of how I heard of Saint Meinrad and decided to come all the way from Wyandotte, Michigan, can be told elsewhere. The fact was, I was about to be dropped off in this faraway place by my parents, with whom I had pleaded to allow me to come. At this moment, though, out on old State Road 62, coming into town and seeing those awesome towers, I did not have the nerve to let on that I was having misgivings.

In our family, my mother was the most spontaneous. My father was somewhat shy, and perfectly content having Mother take the initiative in social situations.

As we were entering town, Mother announced rather sharply: "This is one phone call I am not going to make." She was referring to the instructions we had been given to use the phone in the lobby to call the Abbey Porter to announce our arrival. My father mumbled from his driver's seat: "Well, I am not going to make it." My older brother, Dick, assured us that he wasn't and I in turn said: "Not me."

We came up the pine tree lined road. The entrance to the place was impressive but a bit intimidating. We parked in front of what we now call Benet Hall. There were no curbs or grass then. We climbed the steps and entered the lobby. The phone was in plain sight. We stood around, silently, for an excruciating length of time, until mother gave in and called. Her move was not out of any great generosity, but was dictated by the fact that she needed to find a rest room. We eventually met Fr. Aemelian Elpers and Fr. Prior Benedict Brown.

The next morning at seven o'clock, they dropped me off in front of the lobby steps and drove off. I stood there alone and very lonely. In time Fr. Aemelian came.

I am now aware that that was a defining moment in my life, a major gravitational shift had taken place. I have no regrets.

Pilgrimage of Thanksgiving

This little piece was handwritten and posted on the Marmion Abbey bulletin board on the occasion of the funeral of Fr. Columban Reed, O.S.B.

I asked for permission to represent Saint Meinrad at the funeral of Fr. Columban for very personal reasons. I wanted to write large on the rites of these days my gratitude to Father for the instrumental role he played in the mystery of my vocation as a monk and priest. Our lives touched closely for only a few days, now over 56 years ago, but from that brief encounter, I caromed off to Saint Meinrad and the rest is history and mystery.

Fr. Columban was recruiting for Marmion Military Academy when he stopped at 2515 Biddle Avenue, Wyandotte, Michigan in August of 1936. He had the name of a young graduate from a Catholic boarding grade school, The Hall of the Divine Child, now closed. When he learned that I wanted to go to a seminary, but as yet had made no immediate plans, he stayed and talked Saint Meinrad. Eventually, he made all the arrangements necessary for my enrollment that September.

That brief encounter with his caring ways shaped my life and I shall be forever grateful. My presence here is sign and token for him, for you and for God to see.

Benefactors

Each week at table, a list of benefactors is read out. The community in gratitude wishes to make explicit the names of the people who have contributed substantially to our life and work. Understandably, the names roll off the reader's tongue. In some instances, when the gifts have been recent and notable, most of us will remember. Names like Ruxer, Kemp, Jenn, and Marten are familiar to all of us. Many others are just names in passing to most of us. Each year I hear one that has special meaning to me, and I would like to lift her name off the page and hold her up for just a brief moment for her kindness to the community. Maybe a few others may smile and recall the passing generosity of Miss Anna Casson, when her name is called off in the refectory.

It was in September of 1944 when I got a special call to the office of Fr. Abbot Ignatius. That was a rather awesome thing in those days for a young monk. Suffice it to say, our trips to that office were few and far between and usually were occasions of some moment. Fr. Abbot endeavored to put me at ease. Then he told me of a lady who wished to support a candidate for the priesthood, and he was designating me as the person her money would support.

I had five more school years to go before ordination. I was asked to write to her on occasion and to remember her daily in my prayers. I had a benefactress and she had a name and a face for the person she was educating.

Anna Casson was a retired schoolteacher from New York City. She never saw Saint Meinrad. She told me she couldn't afford the trip out here. After I was ordained, I was sent to Catholic University. Miss Anna picked up the tab for that, as well as for my graduate work in library science later.

On one occasion, with Fr. Abbot's permission, I took the trip from Washington to New York to visit her. How memorable it is to me still. This little old lady, whose face I cannot conjure up, took me to a simple supper in a small restaurant, proud as could be of "her young priest." I remember she put a few sugar cubes in her purse for the horse of the milkman who came around her neighborhood every day. She wanted to treat me to something special that was not too expensive. We took a subway ride to the Manhattan Ferry, and for something like ten cents each, we took the ferry out and back.

I never saw her again, but I will be eternally grateful to that little old lady who, from her life savings. set aside some money to pay for my education. I have remembered her faithfully in prayer. Be sure that my face lights up each year in late July when the reader asks our prayer for Miss Anna Casson.

The Angels' Song

It was dark. It was cold. It was Christmas Eve, 1996. The Abbey Church was a black blob in the midst of the debris that had been dragged from its deep recesses. It had been over six months since the voices of the monks had been heard within it. A whispering band of shadows moved across the path from the Archabbey entrance to the church. It was a covey of romantic monks who wanted to sing the angels' song in the Abbey Church on this Christmas night in the year we were exiled from its walls.

We stood, the eight to ten of us who were there, in the plank-covered passageway under the choir. A nervous flashlight was the only light we had. With faces turned up to try to fill the upper spaces, we intoned the lovely melody of the Angels' Song, *Gloria in Excelsis Deo et in Terra Pax Hominibus Bone Voluntatis.* The melody, by the way, is presumed to have come from Einsiedeln. Copies were lost in the fire in 1887. The story is that Fr. Anselm Maier, O.S.B., wrote down the melody from memory. In any case, the song has been sung in the monastery corridors by members of the schola each Christmas since.

It would be nice to report that the sound reverberated beautifully off the walls of the church. The truth is, a giant fan, which blew hot air with a mighty roar, swallowed up the sound. It was the thought that counted. The little group moved back to the monastery, not exactly elated, but happy for the romantic effort, made in the cold, dark night of Christmas, to praise God in the sacred space so important to their lives as monks.

The Marine Hymn

I was startled in the early hours of the night to hear someone whistling the Marine Hymn on the walkway just outside the east wing of the old monastery. There was no doubt in my mind where it was coming from. Under normal circumstances, I would have been delighted, but insecure as I was, I was afraid I would get in trouble if it woke up some of the more tight-lipped members of the community. When I think of it now, I am embarrassed that I was so uptight. It was a moment to bring a smile to one's face and warmth to the heart.

You see, it was my younger brother, Tom, who was whistling. For some years, the Marine Hymn has been his "trademark." He whistled it a lot while walking, but especially as he got near home. It told my mother that he was on his way. Before she ever heard it, Keno, our dog, had picked it up and began running around like mad until the door was opened and he could dash down the street to meet Tom. Even though I was far from home, here at Saint Meinrad, I knew the story, and I had even experienced the event myself during vacations before I had joined the monastery.

There I was in the silence of my cell listening to my brother greeting me from outside the wall. Instead of reveling with joy at the kindness of his personal signal, I was more absorbed in consequences that I might experience. As usual, there were no consequences. I worried unnecessarily, but worse, missed the sweetness of the moment that a carefree, loving brother provided me.

I never hear the Marine Hymn that I do not think of Tom, and now at a later date, have come enjoy the thought of a young man with an open heart greeting his older brother in the silent dark by whistling the Marine Hymn.

Karen's Story

I was coming from I know not where, when I met Karen. Actually, I can hardly say I met her. She was an airline stewardess, and she stopped at my aisle seat to talk about the book I was reading. It was as simple as that.

I was reading Godden's *In the House of Bred*, a novel about a Benedictine community of nuns in England. The book was well written and incidents authentically portrayed. The book had been publicized by a recent TV production of the story. Karen had seen the program. She asked about the book. When I assured her that the book was well written and that the play had followed it closely, she left me saying she was going to try to get a copy and read it.

I am a Roman Catholic priest. She could tell by my clothes that I was a priest. She figured I might know something of nuns and convents. She could hardly know I was a monk of many years, familiar with community living so dramatically portrayed in the book. How could she have known that I was also a librarian for some 25 years that day when she knelt by my side to talk about the book? The two or three me's within my head and heart began a rather heated discussion on whether I should just continue my reading as if no intrusion had been made in my life, or whether this was a moment of grace. Should I offer to get her a copy, indeed to lend her the one I was reading?

I won't bore you with the details of the argument. In the end, I waited until all had left the plane. I gave her the book with my name and address in the back pocket. I asked her to return the book when she had finished reading it. The way her face lighted up was worth the airfare—round trip, and a very special grace.

After a month or so passed without hearing from her, I resigned myself to a lost book. But then, shortly after, back it came, and like bread on the waters, two more she sent along as gifts. One was *All Things Great & Small* by James Herriot, which introduced me to that gifted writer and began what eventually became a series by him, on our library shelves. Her letter was charming. She had enjoyed the book. She went on to tell me about herself and her zest for life, beginning a casual correspondence that continued for the next couple of years.

I always watched for her when I took the Delta flights. In vain did I search for her recognizing smile. I never saw her again.

On one occasion, I was to be on about five Delta flights in a two-or three-week period. I wrote my full schedules, including layovers in Atlanta. I had hoped we might have coffee and talk. I watched eagerly. Wasn't really sure I'd recognize her face unless she came up to me. I talked about her throughout my trips. I told family and friends I was hoping to meet again the young lady who had knelt by my side and had spoken with such joy of her intent to read a story about women of faith.

On returning home, I found a letter to me from her mother. It should have been edged in black. She thanked me for my interest in Karen, and then went on in some detail to explain the struggle with depression Karen had suffered in recent months. She lost the struggle and took her life. Karen was gone. Her mother pleaded with me to continue to be considerate to other mothers' daughters, the ladies who help us fly the skies, but who may not as yet have their feet on the ground. She thanked me for the personal attention I had given Karen.

Later, sleepless, in the quiet early morning hours I penned this lament for Karen.

Gone now.
Whither? Why?

Who stole the light from Karen's eye?
What secret hand sealed the smile so sweet to me?
Who blew in her ear
    The cloud
That hid the sun from her inner view?
Did some silent prick leave poison
    Festering unto death
    In the folds of her sweet flesh?

What waste that her fragrant womb
    Will never bloom
    Another like to her.

So young, so beautiful, my Karen,
    And yet so burdened
    By life's mysteries!

Could you not have borne the latter
　　For the former delights?

O Karen, dear, what have you solved?
　　What has this snuffing out resolved?

There are mysteries still
　　And pain the more for your passing.

Perhaps saddest of all—
　　Had you but known
　　The long list of those who grieve your passing,
　　You would be with us still.

Kind words unspoken,
Warm embrace not given,
Love left unexpressed
　　May well have left less unnatural
　　The unnatural deed
By which we lost sweet Karen.

Letters of Love

This article about my Mother was written for Marriage and Family Living maga-zine, May 1987.

The postman lost a friend the other day when a little old lady passed away. The mailbag on his shoulder may seem just as heavy, but it's actually a bit lighter. For, through the years, this gentle little lady stretched her caring concern for others like fingers across the country through little notes of love. Not much on style, her sentences were sometimes incomplete and improperly punctuated, but her tender messages always spoke louder than the words themselves. I know; she was my mother.

Actually, it's been some time since she scribbled her little notes and sent them around the country. Mother was on the receiving end these past few years. What joy the bread she cast on the waters brought back to her.

Sometimes, she'd ask me to type a poem for her—a nosegay—that she particularly liked and wanted to share with someone. I almost got to know by heart the one I typed up with carbons most often. It was a simple little verse of positive thinking.

On this day...

Mend a quarrel,
Search out a forgotten friend.
Dismiss a suspicion,
And replace it with trust.
Write a letter to someone
Who misses you.
Encourage a youth
Who has lost faith.
Keep a promise.
Forget an old grudge.

Examine your demands on others
And vow to reduce them.
Fight for a principle.
Express your gratitude.
Overcome an old fear.
Take two minutes
To appreciate
The beauty of nature.
Tell someone you love him;
Tell him again,
And again,
And again.

So closely does this characterize my memory of her that I want to share it. Maybe it'll encourage you to begin such a hobby of love. Take up a pen, as my mother so often did, and burden the mailman. You'll lighten someone's heart.

Cleaning out My Cell

I am on another small journey inward. I have a way of dramatizing the minutiae of my life, but it helps me cope. As I try to cope, someone else may find encouragement to make an inner journey of moves they are being called on to make. I hope at least someone can relate to this mini-drama.

I have been asked by my superior to vacate the room I have been living in for the past 20 years so that it can be used for other purposes. He is perfectly within his rights and I accept the order with a good deal of peace.

The move, however, is challenging me to downsize the belongings that clutter "my house." The following is a quote from a letter on the subject:

I have been asked to move into another cell. I am using the process as another spiritual journey of sorts. I am letting go of an accumulation of stuff over the years. Each item or page has its story as a part of my life, but no one else would give a hoot. So I am squeezing them out and tossing them.

It is a custom here, as perhaps everywhere, that when a monk dies, his door is locked. Fr. Abbot may look through things. The archivist is ordered to look, then the librarian. After that, the house prefect cleans out the room, discarding most of the contents. If something is thought to be of value to someone else, such items are placed on a table in the calefactory for anyone to pick up.

Monks who have died do not see this final step. I get to watch my precious items being pawed over, taken or rejected. Some of my stuff is now in other cells. Some of it went quickly. I suspected some went too quickly and I found them in the trash barrel. Someone must have felt it was an insult to put them out. It is a judgment call. I felt a little wounded, but it put my detachment to the test.

I had a guitar, two clarinets, a metronome, and lots of music. I hadn't played the guitar in years, and the chromatic harmonica dating from the '30s hadn't been touched in years, but parting with that section of my life was like a kind of lobotomy.

The same way with my calligraphy tools, pens, pencils, pads of special paper and practical booklets on the art itself. I had spent about three years using what free time I could spare practicing. I had a dream of promoting a manuscript book of the Gospels for special feasts. I never presumed I would do the book, but I wanted to make the effort at a stab at it to encourage the more skilled among us to do the job. The last piece I did was the Gospel for the Easter Vigil. It was a decent piece, and was used by the deacon. Actually, I did not see it in use, as I had been sent to Fort Knox for pastoral service that weekend. That having been done, I lost all interest and have not taken up any of those tools since, and that is over 20 years ago. I kept thinking that I might take it up again when I got older. I am older and I see no sign of change. It is time to let go.

I have also cleared my bookshelves of what I have considered essential tools, Dictionary of Theology, Bible Atlas, German Dictionary, Jerome Biblical Commentary, homily manuals, books by Marmion, etc. I put out about 15-20. I am pleased to see that most of them are gone. I am not giving up all study or homily preparation, but I can get access to the tools I need in the library.

I do not think I have been excessively attached to my stuff, but it was a part of me, and my past. It hurts a little to sever myself from my past, but I will be traveling lighter. Hopefully, parting with such "friends" may ease the later stages of my journey to eternity.

Well, you get the idea. Forgive these musings of an old man trying to keep a young heart.

Reconciled

I am a monk in a Benedictine monastery. My sister, a religious with the Sisters of the Immaculate Heart of Mary in Monroe, MI, recently spent the long Thanksgiving weekend here. We visited, reminisced, and shared our stories of hopes, dreams, disappointments, and joys. It was a lovely time. Actually, it was the first time she had come alone for visit, though she had been here before with companions. It became a very special time. We are both happy in our vocations. That is not say we are not still facing dilemmas and decisions that can affect substantially the quality of our lives. Our being able to talk things out together was very supportive for both of us.

A few days after my sister left, I came across a bit of doggerel verse written by my father 40 years ago. I had completely forgotten it. Saved on scrap of fading paper, it had been salted away in a box with personal mementoes. I remember well that our leaving home for our respective vocations had been a burden for both our parents. I had forgotten that my father had put his thought in verse.

14

Perhaps when I was younger, they had not meant as much to me, though they are among the very few lines from him, now long gone, that I still preserve. Coming upon them now, when my sister and I have both completed over 40 years in religion, they take on special meaning.

Let me add, we were not his only children. An older brother was serving our country in a war for peace when father penned these lines. Another son was still at home and was a source of much joy in their lives for the rest of their days. It is safe to say, though, this man of faith took special satisfaction in the religious vocations of the boy and girl who became a monk and nun. He revealed as much despite the pain in the verses he titled, "Reconciled."

> Our little girl has left us,
> She aspires to be a nun.
> When you consider a vocation,
> Can you think of a better one?
>
> Our little boy has left us too,
> He to be a monk doth aspire,
> And after careful consideration
> Can you think of a nobler desire?
>
> Yes, Mom and I are lonely,
> And our home has had a sober air,
> But that these kids prove worthy,
> Shall always be our prayer.
>
> God grant that they are successful.
> And when their goals are won,
> Please, God, make us worthy parents
> Of a holy monk and nun.
>
> —*Philip T. Daly*
> *July or August 1943*

My father's words touch me deeply as I read them now. I am consoled that, before he and Mother died, they seemed to enjoy the consolation for which he had prayed in these verses so many years ago.

Fr. Simeon Daly, O.S.B.
February 2, 1985

P.S. Around that same time, that is 1943, knowing their distress, I had penned the following lines.

> Tis almost cruel for God
> To snatch by love
> What by love you held so dear.
>
> Let your hearts beat strong again
> And you will find
> That there entwined
> Are the hearts you grieved as lost.
> They're there in all life power
> Loving and sharing your every hour.

The Engagement of John and Angela Daly

I wrote this in the first person, as if John himself was writing it. It was my little tribute to him.

I am seventh in a family of eight, but I am the last to marry. Some were beginning to wonder if it would ever happen. Especially after the oldest of my brothers and sisters, at the age of 40, finally took the plunge. Believe me, I have felt the pressure and had begun to wonder myself if I would ever find the "girl of my dreams."

Actually, that is not entirely true, because by the time Tom got married a year ago, I had already made up my mind whom I was going to ask to share my life with me. In fact, at that time, I had already spent a year with that conviction. That is not to say, though, that there were not many years of anguish over making the proper choice, a choice I have felt so crucial to the story of my life. I had struggled deep within my heart to find that "significant other" person to share my life with and to be the mother of our children. I made up my mind two years ago. I have been comfortable with my choice throughout this period. I have waited till now to ask her in order to allow her the time she would need to know me, and to have the time and maturity to work out her own decision. She was only 18 when I made mine. I would wait till she was 21 before I would ask her to make hers. No one can say now that I was robbing the cradle, nor that I have jumped into this without sufficient reflection. It was a long wait, to the dismay of family and friends, but I'm glad, now that it is over, that I gave so much time and energy to finding the person who will share so intimately and significantly the rest of my life.

The "courting of Angie" is another story. One, I might add, worth telling. Maybe I'll get to that some day. Right now, though, I just want to capture a few of the details that made the engagement moment so significant for me.

There had been great acts to follow. I have heard the stories of the engagement moments of seven of my brothers and sisters, and scores of others whose lives I've shared down through the years. All my best friends have married before me. I had rehearsed in my mind over and over again what I would say and where I would say it. After all, my brother had proposed to Angie's sister in church before the crib after Christmas midnight Mass. Not that I felt pressured by one-upmanship. I just wanted it to be a meaningful moment. In the end, I opted for the element of surprise. How do you surprise someone you've courted for two years?

I had already bought the ring. It was burning a hole in my pocket. Angie's 21st birthday was approaching. She would have had to be a bit slow not to have figured I would pop the question either on her birthday or shortly thereafter. Angie is not slow. But she was totally blown away when I proposed to her, on a walk in blue jeans, after an ordinary dinner date a week before her birthday. It was no ordinary moment. The tears she shed were tears of joy, which made so memorable this engagement for which I had hoped and prayed for so many years. I'll treasure ever the joy we shared that night. No words can tell the peace and satisfaction I enjoyed knowing I had brought so much happiness to one I love so deeply. A lifetime of shared love lies before us. We are engaged.

Another Chance

A group of us had gotten together to honor Dr. Joseph Thomas, who had just turned 90. He had given a little talk expressing the usual pleasantries, but his remarks included some rather dire concerns he felt for the direction our society was taking. Anyway, the small group of gathered friends, mostly college professor types, was a bit subdued. We stood around doing what you do at receptions with *hors d'oeuvres* and drinks.

I was talking to a colleague. Both of us were rattling ice cubes, though neither of us had anything stronger than a Coke. I brought up the topic of the death the day before of a 10-year-old girl. It happened after the first day of school. A vivacious child, she had waved and shouted her good-byes to one and all, flew out the door, around the front of the bus, right into the path of an oncoming car. The bus driver looked on in sheer horror. We were expressing our concern for the different ones. Regret for the little girl. Compassion for her family and friends. And distress for the young lady, 16 years old, who was at the wheel of the killer car.

She had just gotten her driver's license. She had purposely stayed home late that morning, missing the bus, so she could drive to school. Now school was out and she was heading home with a carload of classmates. She failed to stop, though the school bus signals were all out and functioning. I was saying how horrible it must be for her, no matter how careless she may have been in the fateful moment. My companion became quite pensive and then said forcefully: "She won't get a second chance!"

He went on to explain that, no matter what the courts might say or do, she will live with the tragedy for the rest of her life. Then, quite spontaneously, he added: "I got a second chance." I am always struck by how peak moments make it easy to bare our souls. My friend went on to tell me this story.

"I was in college at the time and quite given to heavy drinking. I was living in West Virginia, at the time, where mountain roads were like corkscrews and valleys short and narrow. I drove intoxicated more than I care to admit. One night, a particularly nasty one, I had made the usual round with friends. I was driving, loaded. I had dropped off my last companion and headed for home over those treacherous roads. I could remember dropping off my buddy at his home. The very next thing I knew, I was walking up the path to my house. Blackout!—The great horror of a heavy drinker. How I had made that dangerous drive home, I'll never know, but I was quick to express my gratitude. Before I entered my house, I said: "Thank you, Lord! You've given me another chance; I'll never do that again."

Then he held up his little paper cup and said: "That's why I only drink this. I have not taken alcohol since. You see now my great sympathy for the young lady whose car took a life. I had a second chance. She won't."

Music in the Park

Since the spring of 1992, in one place or another, a small group of monks has been practicing band music together. Membership has waxed and waned like the phases of the moon, but has kept a solid core. For the past two years, they have practiced in the old wine cellar, a place remote enough to muffle the sound for sensitive ears. Their recent eviction from there, for reasons not pertaining to music committed, was the occasion of the recent Sunday afternoon concert in the monastery gazebo (September 24, 1995). Protests were not violent, so they tried it again on October 1, to help celebrate the first major visit of the Benedictine sisters of Ferdinand to our community. The weather was pleasant, and from reports the music was appreciated by most. Weather permitting, the band plans to do its Sunday sessions in the gazebo starting next Sunday at 1:30.

Present band members are: Br. Lawrence, Br. Vincent, Fr. Simeon, Br. Terence and this fall, Fr. Jack Bendik. Membership is open. New members regularly sought. Some knowledge of music required, but obviously not much.

One might note for the record that Fr. Kevin, now on leave from the band, Fr. Dunstan, retired, and Br. Vincent provided the motivation and energy to launch this project, which has engaged the group in two sessions a week, for over three years, out of the view and hearing of all.

Fr. Simeon Daly, O.S.B.
October 5, 1995

Addendum, March 25, 1998. I regret to say that a serious illness interrupted my participation in June of 1996. Although I returned for a few sessions after about six months, I also retired from being an active player. I cannot adequately describe the slight twinge I get as I hear Br. Lawrence and Br. Vincent patiently persevering, as they continue to play together.

2004: Fr. Dunstan, Br. Lawrence and Br. Vincent have passed away.

Abba Moses

This was written in the genre of the Desert Fathers to try to help address something that arose in a counseling session years ago.

Many years ago, before the riverbeds were dry, when monks lived in caves, a middle-aged monk wandered slowly up the hillside and called on Abba Moses.

"Abba Moses, my Father, will you hear me?"

"Tomorrow I will hear you. Sit here in quiet for a few hours and then we will break bread together. Tomorrow we will speak."

"But I am eager to talk now. I have thought out all I want to say."

"Tomorrow, my son. Now sit in silence and open your heart to God's mercy and to His Spirit."

The monk took this as some kind of rebuke, but as time passed, his heart grew lighter. A great calm came over him as he felt the strength of the great Abba Moses across from him in prayerful silence.

After some hours, Abba Moses brought out bread and grapes and water and the two men shared many things together. Next morning, the monk told his story with simple candor.

"Some years ago," he started, "I got very much behind in filling orders for baskets and my work began to be oppressive. After some seeking for help, a young lady of exceeding discipline and skill came to weave with me. I immediately determined to extend to her my love as Jesus would have me do. I have done this now these many years."

"Are you not at peace over this good work?" Abba Moses asked.

"Yes, but also a bit uneasy. I want to say some things and I don't know how to do so without sounding condescending."

"Will she listen to you?"

"That, too, worries me. In some way I fear being rejected, but more than that, I fear being misunderstood. In my heart, I love her. I don't want my love to frighten her or distress her."

"What are you trying to say? You're not making any sense to me. Go down the hill for one hour and then come and tell me what's on your mind."

The monk felt rejected, but did as he was told. When he came back, he spoke freely.

"This young lady is a very beautiful person."

"I thought as much, if she has stayed with you and those baskets for so long."

"She is bright and sharp and has a radiant vigor, but I feel she puts herself down. Actually, I feel she has been put down so often that, even though she resists it, she has come to question that she could be lovable."

"That's not so unusual," Abba Moses said. "It seems to me you have had a bit of that yourself. What have you been doing?"

"Each day, in any way I can, I try to affirm her qualities, to help her say 'yes' to her womanhood, to understand that she is loveable and capable."

"Has this been difficult?'

"It has become increasingly easy."

"Why don't you let well enough alone?"

"This puzzles me, too, good Father, and it is why I seek your counsel. I want to love her unselfishly and non-possessively. I want to love her without in any way taking over her life. I want her to feel my love and return it, but I do not want to awaken in her a love for me that might hurt her. I want to remain a monk and weave baskets. I want her to be able to accept this love, enjoy it, but not be swept up by it. Do you understand what I am saying?"

"I hear you saying you have a lot of wants. I suspect this is running deep in you."

"It does."

"If she is as smart as you say, don't you think she knows all this? Have you ever tried to talk about it?"

"I try in little ways, but feel resistance. Once I told her flat out that I loved her and hoped that my love would give her strength."

"What happened then?"

"She didn't even look up. Just stared at her work and kept on weaving."

"What did that say to you?"

"A number of things, some good and some not so good."

"Like…?"

"Like, 'buzz off kid, you're acting like an adolescent.' Or, 'I hear you and I thank you, but please don't make me respond.' Or 'I feel you're conning me, and I refuse to be conned.'"

"If your love is really unselfish, why do you have to have an answer? If the second one, that she hears you and doesn't want to respond, is true, aren't you right where you would like to be?"

"Yes, but—"

"You are full of 'yes buts.' I would like you better if you were more yes or no."

"Good Father, I wish I were less complicated, too. I think I want her to be comfortable with my love so that she would be open to love anyone else."

"Do you really believe that?"

"Yes I do. I have a feeling she doesn't believe anyone can love her and so she mistrusts a relationship. Like she might be hurt."

"Maybe that's true. Why do you press it? If your love is really healing, let it heal. You go away now and think about that. Come back tomorrow."

Early the next morning, the monk trudged up to the cave again. Abba Moses was waiting. He received the monk warmly and spoke kindly, without the sharpness he had showed the day before.

"My son, I believe you love much, and you are to be commended for the fidelity and perseverance of your love. If I hear you correctly, there are small signs of possessiveness and manipulation in your love. You seem too eager for signs of response. If this young weaver is a sharp as you imply her to be, she knows. Don't play games or make her play games of 'I love you. I love you not.' She has her own life to lead. For whatever reason, she is not verbally responding, but she continues to weave baskets."

Seeing the puzzled look on the face of his counselee, Abba Moses asked, "You have more to say?"

Yes, Father, I would like to embrace her."

"I thought there was something else. What's that supposed to do?"

"Well, nothing much I suppose. At least on special occasions it would seem quite normal."

"Have you just thought of that?'

"Oh no! For several years now."

"And...?"

She seems to cringe from any touch. It is like a deep fear. Of late, there seems more trust. I've been struck how frequently I have embraced or been embraced by others whom I have known but shortly. However, I have spent hours each day and almost every day with her and she still seems so frightened if I'm close. I have a strong desire to reach out to her, to say I care, to say don't be afraid, to say be confident, to..."

"You're disgustingly wordy. Why do you have to say all those things? Why don't you just let her weave baskets, that's what she is there for, isn't it?"

"Yes, but..."

"There goes your 'yes but' again."

"It's so hard to explain, but I'm beginning to see that I am being a bit self-centered by trying to evoke some response, but…"

"Ah, but!"

"I love her as she is and would want her to know."

She knows. Go home. Be as loving and as warm as you normally would be, neither more nor less. Do not ask of her what she is not ready to give and do not confuse your relationship as weaver with petty games. You are fortunate to have a companion who does not seek what she cannot have and does not take advantage of your openness. Learn to listen and to see. She is responding, by her fidelity, by care, by sharing. You are asking too much, and never dare to embrace her unless you know that she says 'Yes!' and that it be an expression of friendship. And even at that, let it be rare, indeed. Now get back to your baskets."

The two embraced warmly and the middle-aged monk left Abba Moses with a light heart and a discernable skip in his step as he made his way back to his cell.

He did what he was told, and said nothing. He and his helper went on weaving baskets, comfortable in each other's presence, neither demanding of the other what he or she could not give.

And it was never known if they ever embraced.

A Moment of Crisis

It is now some years since Fr. Cajetan White died. I trust it is not out of place to reveal a rather private moment in our lives. It is a story that I have shared with very, very few until now.

Fr. Cajetan and I were friends, good friends. Our friendship began back when he was a young monk in the community, before his final vows and ordination. It was music that brought us together. He was an accomplished musician. For years, he had played the organ, but he was partial to flute. We were able to find some music for clarinet and flute, which, over the years, we played together. Sometimes even in church.

He not infrequently came to me for counsel, but for almost 20 years, we worked together in the library. In these encounters, we seldom referred to the fact that he was subject to epileptic moments as a result of an accident he had as a boy. For the most part, it was kept under control by medication.

One morning in the library, he had some rather bizarre body movements that made him look stoned. I suspected immediately that he was having a mild spell. I called Br. Daniel. He asked me to try to get him to his cell and he would stop by to look at him. Trying to help him to his cell was no easy task. He showed no resistance, but he had a hard time keeping his balance, and even putting one foot in front of the other.

Br. Daniel came, assessed that it was indeed a small episode of his epileptic condition, and prescribed bed rest for the rest of the day.

I came and went throughout the day just to see if he were all right. After my own supper, I went to check to make sure a tray had been brought to him. It had, and he was in the process of eating as I came in. I sat in his chair and we visited on a very superficial level. Without being quite sure when it began, I noticed that he seemed to be choking. How many moments it was that I continued to sit there, I do not know, but I suddenly became convinced that he was in real trouble. I was wearing my habit at the time, I remember. It wasn't very decorous, but I jumped up on his bed, got him turned around on his side and performed the "Heimlich Maneuver," forcing his diaphragm in and up. After the second or third try, he spit out a rather large piece of meat that had stuck in his throat. Perhaps it was the awkwardness of cutting up the meat in bed or defective muscle action that brought on the problem. We were both convinced that, without my action, late though it was, he would have choked to death.

I have had no other comparable experience in my life. He lived a good number of years after that before he lost his life in a more severe epileptic attack.

May he rest in peace.

Unnecessary Concern

Fr. Theodore has a cell immediately next to mine. Although he can walk for short distances, he uses a battery-operated cart to get around. Fr. Theodore is 102 years old. He is always early for any service and follows a rather consistent routine of coming and going from his cell. Although I do not set my watch by it, I notice whether the cart is outside his door or not.

It so happened I was rushing to get to church on time one afternoon, when I was stunned to see his cart in place. At first, I was going to ignore it, but I thought he might need help. He would normally be in church for more than five minutes by now.

I knocked on his door and went in. He was seated at his desk reading. He turned and gave me a rather perplexed look, like "what are you doing here?" After I had pointed out the time and he didn't make a move, I concluded rather hastily that he must be slipping. It saddened me to see his slow response to my concern. He said, "I planned on coming a little later." "But, Father," I said, "It is three minutes to five." Finally, after a few moments of indecision, he said that he would come. I hurried off just a little saddened by the developments.

When I got to the slype, the monks were not lined up to enter church as they would normally be before Saturday Vespers. Only then did it dawn on me that this was the eve of Palm Sunday. As has been the custom in recent years, the community and guests had gathered in front of the lobby for the blessing of Palms and procession into church, a ceremony that takes about 15 minutes. Now it dawned on me that Fr. Theodore had been trying to get in a few more pages of reading. It was too late for me to join the community. I simply sat in choir rather stunned that, in trying to watch over an old man, I had betrayed my own inattentiveness to the schedule.

My aged confrere, 21 years my senior, was more alert to the situation than I. It was a bit humbling, but a nice moment for all of that.

The Yoke of Obedience

One's perspective of major moments of his or her life can shift over time. The drudgery of preparing for an exam turns into euphoria at a job well done when it is over. I recall a particular personal struggle I experienced as a young monk that I now look back on as time of grace. It was an interior struggle. I doubt that anyone else was aware of it. I record it now for the insight it provides to a stage in my own life. It may serve as an example of how perspectives of a given moment can change over time.

In our formation years, the young monastics of our house were encouraged to take some preliminary preparation for possible future higher studies. The superiors tried to respect preferences of individuals. Small groups of workshops were conducted in the various disciplines: theology, literature, church history, Scripture, etc. Of course, not all of us could major in the area of our own choice. We understood that. However, it was a genuine effort to stimulate interest in higher studies. I was in the Scripture group. Of the five or six in our group, only Fr. Martian Strange was assigned to go on in Scripture. He eventually got a doctorate in sacred theology, a licentiate in sacred Scripture, and a master's degree in Oriental languages.

Right after Ordinations, the fall semester of 1948, Fr. Kenneth Wimsatt and I went to Catholic University for a licentiate in sacred theology. He went on to Toronto for further studies in theology. I returned home to teach. I taught religion in the Minor Seminary and liturgy in the Major Seminary (1949-1950). During the first semester, I was assigned to help in the Abbey Library. In November, I was appointed to the library staff. Later I went back to Catholic University for a degree in library science.

Some years later, when Fr. Kenneth was teaching theology and I was head librarian, I experienced some pangs of jealousy. He was able to spend many hours in the library studying and preparing for his classes. He was a most serious and diligent student. Frequently, it was incumbent on me to provide material for his study. It grated on me that I was busy about many things in the library, stamping books, filing cards, etc., while he got to spend countless hours reading theology. The true demand of obedience came home to me as never before. I was to work

30

out my salvation by making sure that others had what they needed to work out theirs. Slowly, the supernatural point of view took over and I was at peace again, making it my joy to serve Fr. Kenneth, and others as well.

I hope I reveal this anguishing moment of my life for no other reason than to bear witness to a time of struggle and grace in my life. What was at first a heavy burden became a work of joy and peace. The external circumstances did not change at all. The shift was in my head and heart. The shift in my perception of what was going made all the difference in the world. For my part, I embraced my role as librarian and had a long, happy and fruitful career.

Letters to and from Mary

This is fiction with a basis in fact. Mary is a chosen name to protect the innocent.

February 22, 1985

Dear Mary,

It's 3 a.m. I'm on a sick bed. Sleepless. Having thought of you, I wondered again what the meaning of your change of address could possibly be. A simple word from you could have clarified that. Without such clarification, my sleepless mind was free to cover a number of scenarios that I have imagined in the form of possible letters from you. The style intrigues me, even if it seems to demean or manipulate you. Take what follows as a literary exercise that normally would have been stifled in its opening moments by virtuous discipline or frazzled fatigue. Full of chemicals, I am not fully responsible for what follows.

Possible letter #1

Dear Simeon,

Now that I have a few moments, I want to explain what must have seemed a mystery to you, my move back to the convent and out of the hospital. I gambled and lost. It's as simple as that. There were some god-awful moments and some miserable days and nights, but I am beginning to feel whole again. There was no way I could put this down on paper until now.

I tried to discharge one of our senior staff doctors. I was justified in my own mind that this was a move for the benefit of the hospital and our patients. I started by suggesting to him that he resign. He is 60 years old, no longer dedicated, financially independent. He could retire gracefully and I need not disclose complaints of harassment, absenteeism, and some questionable medical decisions. What started out as a calm exchange soon became a nasty scene. I had no idea of the hornet's nest I had opened up. He challenged me then and there. One of us would go. It turned out to be me. By the time I tried to pursue the issue through normal channels, he had whipped up such a political maelstrom that I

32

had no chance. Raw political power is nothing short of awesome. Newspapers, radio, and TV were manipulated in his favor and against me with such skill that I lost all credibility with my board and with the public. At first, I was determined to fight, but the futility of it all was soon impressed upon me, and for the sake of the hospital I felt it best to resign. I am confident that the doctor will resign soon. He knows my charges were true.

I have twinges of regret for sure. I will bear the scars of this for a long time, but I'll manage. I'm a survivor. More later.

Mary

Possible letter #2

Dear Simeon,

I don't believe I told you. On November 22, my community elected me superior. I can't say I was totally surprised by the action. A number of indications of sentiment were communicated to me earlier on. I tried not to resist, though I pointed out the minor crisis that would develop at the hospital. While we have other nurses, no one in the community is really qualified to take my place. Needless to say, I have inherited that problem. I am keeping the title of administrator but have turned over the work to a qualified layman until Sister Dorothy can complete her internship as an administrator at St. Luke's.

At Christmas, I didn't have time to explain all this. You can understand now the cryptic note about the January 10th change of address. So far, everyone has been most kind. Fortunately, I had kept close contact with the Motherhouse. I do not feel at all the stranger as I pick up on daily routines. Truth to tell, I like the change. I'll know better after a year or so if it was a wise decision.

Keep me in your prayers.

Mary

Possible letter #3

Dear Simeon,

I'm back at the convent as you noted I would be. In my earlier note, I simply wasn't up to explaining what was going on at the time. Now, I somehow need to.

I need to talk to someone away from here, just to feel free to let it all hang out for a few minutes anyway. Can you allow me that?

Needless to say, I presume you will. I feel you will understand me when I try to convey the devastation that I have experienced. Everyone here, of course, knows and tries to be understanding, but I feel I'm off in a world by myself. I want to get back into their world, but I can't force it; neither can they. I am determined not to let my life be ruined. I hope just walking through this experience will help me inch my way back toward wholeness and sanity. Bear with me.

On December 13th, in a small anteroom in the basement of the hospital around 11 p.m., I was raped by an assailant. I had been to a dinner meeting with friends of the hospital, planning for a fund-raising campaign. Although I was slightly aware I was being followed from my car to the back entrance, I was not frightened or panicky. After I had turned the key in the door, which is kept locked all the time for security, a gloved hand reached over my shoulder and covered my hand still holding the key in the lock. A man whispered: "Keep going" and "quietly." I already felt violated. I never dreamed terror could be so debilitating. What strength I had drained out of me. There was a small room just inside the back door. Before the renovation, this had been the emergency entrance. He wanted money. I really believe that's all he wanted, but when all I could give him was the $2.46 in my purse, he was livid with rage. Had I had $50 or $100, I believe he would have taken it and left. But he didn't. I could almost see the decision developing. It was not born of lust; it was a violent expression of raw anger.

What happened, happened quickly. I can't believe how quickly and, despite my feeble resistance, how efficiently he did what he did. In one way, it's all a blur to me now. It couldn't have taken more than a few minutes. When I deal with it that way, it is more tolerable. Most of the time, though, the scene and all its violence moves slowly across my memory—slow motion—stop slide by stop slide, as if I had photographed and tape-recorded each passing second. It seems to take hours to run by, and I relive the horror and terror of those cruel moments with their rawest pain. The unforgettable violence he did to my body, with all the physical hurt that accompanied it, is nothing to the violence he has done to my mind. He so violated me there that I feel him as real as if he had stuck a stick in my skull. I know I tried to scream while it happened, but I never hear the scream as I rerun the screen. That scream is still in me, and I know sometime before long I'm going to have to go somewhere and get it out. I just have this feeling that when I do, I'll begin to get some control over this thing that intrudes on my every waking and sleeping hour.

I never had the slightest idea of how unraveling a rape can be. Hardly a day passes that I don't see another one reported. Only the victims have any idea how totally violated they are. As bleak as this sounds though, Simeon, I am mending. Each day I notice the distancing that is taking place. I never expect to escape completely, but I do hope, as time goes on, to pick up on friends and responsibilities again. For the moment, I'm satisfied to try to establish a little distance between reruns when the heavy breathing starts and I listen carefully for the silent scream that accompanies the physical actions that have so devastated my spirit.

It helped to get this all out. Sorry if it sounds heartless. My heart is on hold for a while. Let me hear from you, and let's both hope that when we next meet this unnerving memory will have begun to fade.

Mary

Possible letter #4

Dear Simeon,

Would you believe, we are experiencing a freeze here. Happens only every ten or twenty years. The scene is lovely to look at; it belies the damage taking place all around. Poor people, ill prepared for so sharp a cold, are suffering frostbite and even freezing to death as the relentless chill stalks the countryside. We are suffering from the cold, but nothing like some of our neighbors.

I'm writing because I want to share something with you. I have been through a most difficult period in my life, and many of my feelings have been numbed as fully as this cold is numbing bodies all around. I have good friends here, and they are helping me hold my life together. For all of that, I'm feeling very lonely tonight. Forgive me if I sound too sorry for myself. I need to air some of these feelings and I have been thinking of writing you for some time anyway to explain my change of address. When last I wrote, I could not bring myself to tell you what was really going on.

I'm three months pregnant and having quite a time just coping with the physiological and psychological changes that wash over me like relentless waves. It's one thing to read about it, or in nurses' training, to rattle off concomitant symptoms that accompany pregnancy; and quite another to experience the nausea, the fantasies, the highs and the lows that go with the real thing. Of course, all this is compounded for me because of my religious principles. I am constantly humbled by the awareness that I have been unfaithful to my vows.

Obviously, something happened. And now, from the distance I have been able to make from the episode, there was in it all, like everything else, a beginning, a middle and an end. The beginning seems long and drawn out. The middle and end converge almost into the same time frame. I'm getting ahead of myself. Let me walk through what happened, as I perceive it now. I trust you not to be too judgmental, though I don't defend my actions. Maybe talking it through will help me. My head and my heart are not yet at one on this. I know what happened was wrong—at least on one level. I am not yet able to repudiate the surge of love that I experienced for another human being. There was something divine about that. I just haven't sorted it all out yet. Can you understand what I am saying?

The relationship was ordinary enough at first. Our work at the hospital brought us together on numerous occasions. I began to notice a slight change just a year ago at the time. I think I noticed it in my own body before I realized that he was maneuvering meeting, extending conversations, making small occasions when our hands touched. Our eyes frequently met. I grew to appreciate how much affection and concern can be shown with the eyes. Because we were of one mind on so many of our professional concerns, it became increasingly comfortable to be with him, given the sometimes-hostile environment of the hospital. Actually, last summer when you and I talked, I almost brought him up. By then our relationship was close and getting closer, and I knew, as I'm sure he knew, that we would have to deal with that. It was weird in a way. We both knew, but we seemed somehow to hold the guilt of it off by not speaking of the absorbing preoccupation we developed for one another. Would you believe, that night we had both, independently of one another, decided to discuss the implications of our relationship and to find ways to preserve our friendship without the possession of one another that was beginning to take place. That night we made love to one another. In the maelstrom that followed that embrace, in a mixture of joy and sorrow, of fulfillment and betrayal, of guilt and joy, in one another's arms, we decided this should not, could not go on. What a surprise it was to each of us to discover the battle the other had been waging. It was the same for both of us. What we were doing was wrong, was against our stated life values and yet—and yet, it seemed so right and so good to love and be loved at such a profound level. Before we parted that night, we had set limits for ourselves that we have religiously observed since.

Isn't it ironic, what has come to pass? Although a fleeting thought of a possible pregnancy twinged my mind, I really had put it so completely out of my mind that I was unprepared to notice the little physical signs that might have prepared me for the diagnosis when it came. What a couple of days those were, Simeon!

My doctor was shocked. She was even more surprised to comprehend that I was surprised. I don't have to tell you all the things that ran pell-mell through my head. Joy, anger, suicide, abortion, delight, up and down, in and out, over and over. My head and my heart were seldom on the same wavelength. The thoughts kept cascading, as difficult to catch hold of as any waterfall.

That was all just after the Christmas and New Year celebrations. Needless to say, it was a very low period for me. As time passed, one by one, decisions have been made and I will live with them. I will stay here for another month. Then I well discretely depart. I will continue to remain in the community. Put the baby up for adoption, and make the most of the life I have left. I am sorry for what I have done that was wrong, but I do not regret that the rich love I experienced generated life.

I'll keep you posted. Thanks for listening and understanding.

Mary

Well, Mary, there it is, the meandering of a tired mind pondering in different ways the meaning of the cryptic bit of information scribbled on an envelope. My illness provided the leisure, though I feel a bit guilty for the hours it took to write it down. It was all done within the course of one day, taking in all about three to four hours. I'll not take the time to copy or edit it. After all, it was meant as a bit of frivolity. I got carried away from my original idea of simply hinting at various scenarios.

In any case, I offer this for your eyes with some hesitation. Perhaps, I have been too free and you may be offended by the way I presume to walk around in your head. No offense is intended, truly!

Do let me hear from you. And soon. I will be anxious until I do.

Simeon

Dear Simeon,

I wasn't quite sure how to take your scenarios. I read them with some detachment and found them interesting. I would be less than honest if I didn't tell you that I have some mixed feelings. I trust you did not intend them to be insulting. What an eerie feeling I had as I read them. Kind of scary what you can do with words!

As to the reason for my change of name and address, you guessed.

Mary

The Visit

I want to record a special visit. This is not a story with a crash ending, but one that I would like to record.

For some years now, I have been taking medicine to thin my blood. The theory is that, should my heart go into fibrillation, the thinned-out blood will be less apt to coagulate in the bottom of the malfunctioning heart. The danger of such coagulation is that a blood clot might be forced into the system, causing a stroke or a heart attack. I had been duly warned of this possibility. I was not unduly distressed about my condition, but when I was in intensive care after surgery in November of 1995 and my heart began thumping about 160 times a minute, I watched the monitor with more anxiety than I care to admit. At that particular time, I had been off the anticoagulant for two weeks. Presumably, there was a strong potential for clotting.

I have come to be more relaxed about my condition in the time since. I have had a half a dozen or more of such episodes. While I am still aware of dire possibilities, I am not so much alarmed when it occurs. Time and experience have tempered my fears.

It so happened that on that Friday afternoon in November, I was expecting a visit. A lady with whom I had worked for almost ten years had promised to come. I looked forward to her visit, both because I was somewhat lonely in the hospital, but, also, because her friendship is very special to me. I was lodged somewhere in the inner workings of the Intensive Care Unit. Fearing that she would have a hard time locating me, I had forewarned all the nurses of her intended visit so they could help her find her way to my bedside. Before she came, my heart began to act up.

The negative images I had developed of my condition put me in considerable distress. When she finally arrived, I was torn between the desire to visit and the dread of her being there and witnessing some trauma. I know I was not able to explain all that to her at the moment. I risked hurting her feelings rather than have her be there to witness me in the throes of a stroke or a heart attack. I kissed her hand and said: "Please go." She went and I cried.

I am not sorry that I was able to think of her feelings in that hour of trial. My memory of my feelings is etched deep in my heart. I remember it as one of my most painful moments.

An Afternoon in Düsseldorf

I don't know how to begin my little story. Many details before and after this special day in my life would help to sharpen its focus and add color. Even of the day itself there could be a longer and shorter version. I'm aiming for the shorter one. The fact is I do not recall ever telling the centerpiece of this story of a day that has so touched my heart and so colored my life. As they say, there is a time to keep silent and a time to speak. Until now, my inner voices have counseled silence. Now, after a near-death experience, I feel my tongue has been loosened. That near-death experience, by the way, was not one of sweetness and light, but a terrible aching abyss at the prospect of having to leave family and friends. Now I feel almost driven to express my thanks for the loves I enjoy. Perhaps I am a bit too eager to express my gratitude. In any case, I know I have been blessed.

It was 1967. I was in Düsseldorf, Germany, on a day's outing with a friend of some nine years at the time. I was 45, and had been a professed monk for 23

years. It was a July day, hot and sultry. Later, in fact it, rained heavily and I like to tell of how we shared a small umbrella. "Gallant" that I was, I held it over both of us, only to learn later that I had protected myself while she was getting drenched. Alas.

It was early afternoon. We were seated on a bench on the bank of the Düssel River. At an appropriate moment, my friend turned to me, looked deep into my eyes and said: "I have a confession to make." Until this moment of my relating this event to you, I have not thought of what must have been going through her mind. What risk was she taking in speaking out? Would I shrivel up and fade away? Would I, perhaps, at the other extreme, fall into her arms, and thereby create havoc for both of us? She was risking a lot and being very trusting when she told me of her love for me. I was not totally surprised that she cared for me deeply. After all, I was not blind, deaf or insensitive. I was a little stunned, though, that she expressed herself so explicitly. After a few brief but awkward moments, I said: "By a cruddy, cruddy stream she professed her love for me." We both broke up. The tension was broken. With ease, we spoke of our mutual love. Although she knew it, I quite properly explained to her that while I had feelings, much the same as hers, I also had commitments as a celibate monk and priest that I wished ever to honor. I accepted her love and proffered mine within those parameters.

It has been a mark of our friendship in the almost 30 years since, that she has never ever embarrassed me, has never tried to possess me, nor take over any aspect of my life. Her love has been generous, unselfish and expansive. I hope I have given in kind. It is fair to say that my day in Düsseldorf that sultry afternoon was a focal point in my life. I remain forever grateful that a friend took a risk in expressing her love for me. We have enjoyed half a life of precious friendship, and I have been a richer person for that risk. Thank you, Lois!

Awaiting a Visit on My Seventieth Birthday

These verses were written hastily on the occasion of a visit to the Abbey by Lois for my birthday. It was a playful piece in which I wanted to contrast the young and vibrant greeting of earlier visits with the more labored movements of these latter years...

You come
  With eager longing, I await your visit.

I long for your sweet embrace
  and the warm kiss you will place
  on my expectant lips.

You should no longer expect me, though
  to come racing across the sward
  to leap into your outstretched arms.

The spring has gone from my steps.
  No more gazelle-like can I hurry.
  Rather, I'll lumber like a bear late for hibernation.

Worry not, I'll make good time, as best I can,
  with ready heart for warm embrace
  and kisses too.

Age may bow my body.
  My heart is stronger still.
  I love you, Lois.

Remembering Father Dunstan McAndrews, O.S.B.

In life and in death, Fr. Dunstan was a very colorful person. Many individual stories, told by confreres and former students, weave a pattern of a strong person, a bit bumptious at times, but kind and thoughtful. I myself have many memories. They reveal different aspects of his personality, different facets of his interests. Most of all, I recall his love of music and his willingness to go to any lengths to get a music group going. One of the bright hours of his week in latter days was playing with a small group of monks who tried hard, barely successfully, to make music together. Even when he could no longer walk, and could hardly see, we wheeled him and his baritone horn to wherever we were playing. Were I to try to capture my vision of him I would describe him as a little boy in a big man's body who tried too hard to be graceful, but in his bumbling, fumbling way managed to grace our lives by his wit, by his charm, by his simplicity. He shunned intimacy like the plague, but could not disguise, though he would try, his loving heart of gold.

I had communicated the news of Father's death to my classmates and was touched by a number of responses. One in particular by Raymond Reno, a former student who had not seen Fr. Dunstan for at least 50 years, attested to the deep impression that Father had had in his life. None of us could do justice to the wide variety of his interests, but I thought that Ray communicated well a feel for the Fr. Dunstan we all remember. Here is what he said:

"No one who ever knew him could forget him, and my memories of him are vivid—a big, red-faced man of great energy, with a swashbuckling way of walking—much swinging of meaty arms—and he'd throw his head back when he laughed or told a joke, and he loved jokes. He also had somewhat of a heavy hand in teaching. I got more than a few claps along the side of the head for stupid answers or paying insufficient attention. But there was no malice or cruelty in him. He was, you'll remember, the instructor for the Red Cross life-saving program, and our final test was to dive into the lake and haul him ashore. He didn't make the task easy—just barely possible. Another memory is of his urging us to do at least ten sit-ups a day and promising that if we did, we'd soon have stomachs like washboards—all this from a man whose own stomach was as far from being a washboard as that of the Pillsbury Doughboy! What a grand man he was, though! I'm sure he's deeply missed by everyone at St. Meinrad."

Yes, Ray, he is deeply missed.

Giving

I watch with great interest the weekly reports of the Development Office posted on our bulletin board. It gives in some detail what that office brings in week after week. I continue to be touched by the generosity of so many people who dig deeply into their resources to support Saint Meinrad Archabbey and its works.

It is romantic to credit community support to the small contributions of many people from their moderate means. The truth is we must also rely on the larger donations of people of means. Motivations of givers interest me. Recently I received a note from a very generous gentleman who gives not only of his means but also of his considerable talent. He remarked:

"While I am grateful for my many blessings, including our friendship, I also realize the importance of sharing these blessings with others...My sentiment is inspired by a quote from St. Gregory the Great from his sixth-century commentary on the Gospels—a quote that could have been written just as well for someone like me at the end of the 20th century. 'Nor must we allow the charm of success to seduce us, or we shall be like a foolish traveler who is so distracted by the pleasant meadows through which he is passing that he forgets his destination.'"

In a similar vein, I was impressed by the sentiments of William Duke of Aquitaine. I recently came across the document he prepared on the occasion of his providing the funding for the foundation of Cluny in 910, a Benedictine abbey that went on to become a most important Christian center for religion and culture. Among other things in the document, he says:

"...I...while there is yet time to make provision for my salvation, have found it right...to dispose for the good of my soul of some of the temporal possessions which have been bestowed upon me...I would not wish to deserve the reproach in the hour of my death that I had used them only for the needs of my body, but would rather, when my last moment shall take them all from me, give myself the joy of having used a part for my soul...I, William, with my wife Ingelberge, give these things...first for the love of God, then for the soul of my Lord and King Eudes, for the souls of my father and mother, for me and my wife, that is for the salvation of our souls and bodies..." (Joan Evans. Monastic Life at Cluny 910-1157. London, Oxford University Press, 1931, p. 4, 5)

These were the sincere sentiments of a rich man in the 10th century. They may well be the sentiments of persons today who, for the salvation of their souls, the glory of God and the support of His Church, consider making a gift, large or small, to support the humble efforts of this Benedictine center of religion and culture in the 20th century.

And She May Still Exist...

Over the years, I have heard in speeches or read in articles a quote from Lord Macaulay, a 19th-century statesman and man of letters. The few lines express a colorful metaphor for the longevity of the papacy and perforce the Roman Catholic Church: "And she may still exist in undiminished vigor when some traveler from New Zealand shall, in the midst of a vast solitude, take his stand on a broken arch of London Bridge to sketch the ruins of St. Paul's."

The traveler from New Zealand may well have been an expression of the time representing the improbable. The fact is, his remarks were almost prophetic during the World War II when bombs fell on London. Fortunately, the London Bridge was spared, but much of London was a ruins much as he described.

I was intrigued by this expression and was delighted to find in one of Msgr. Tracey Ellis' books a footnote that located the original passage. The quoted expression first appeared in the periodical *Edinburgh Review* in 1840 (v.71 p. 228). Bells went off in my head because I remembered that we happen to have a long run of the E. R. in our library. With winged feet (I was much more agile in those days), I hurried to the shelves where, indeed, we had the cited volume. How delighted I was to find the quote. Even more delighted was I to find the whole paragraph of which the above quote was only the concluding sentence. The whole paragraph was one long paean on the vitality of the Roman Catholic Church.

Lord Macaulay was not of the Roman Church, but he had the integrity to give it its due. The full quotation, which I want to share with you, appeared as the third paragraph of his review of Leopold von Ranke's *The Ecclesiastical and Political History of the Popes of Rome, during the Sixteenth and Seventeenth Centuries.* Von Ranke was a Protestant scholar who was the first historian to be given access to the Vatican archives for his study. The review, by the way, was 31 pages long after the manner of the time. I myself have read this passage aloud to others as often as I felt I could impress or edify my hearer. I take great pride in having the volume from 150 years ago in our library, and pride in the pompous praise of the Church. It is beautiful English language. Read it aloud. It almost sings.

"There is not, and there never was, on this earth, a work of human policy so well deserving of examination as the Roman Catholic Church. The history of that Church joins together the two great ages of human civilization. No other institution is left standing, which carries the mind back to the times when the smoke of sacrifice rose from the Pantheon, and when camelopards and tigers bounded in the Flavian amphitheatre. The proudest royal houses are but of yesterday, when compared with the line of the Supreme Pontiffs. That line we trace back in an unbroken series, from the Pope who crowned Napoleon in the nineteenth century, to the Pope who crowned Pepin in the eighth; and far beyond the time of Pepin the august dynasty extends, till it is lost in the twilight of fable. The republic of Venice came next in antiquity. But the republic of Venice was modern when compared with the Papacy; and the republic of Venice is gone, and the Papacy remains. The Papacy remains, not in decay, not a mere antique; but full of life and youthful vigour. The Catholic Church is still sending forth to the furthest ends of the world, missionaries as zealous as those who landed in Kent with Augustin; and still confronting hostile kings with the same spirit with which she confronted Attila. The number of her children is greater than in any former age. Her acquisitions in the New World have more than compensated her for what she has lost in the Old. Her spiritual ascendency extends over the vast countries which lie between the plains of the Missouri and Cape Horn—countries which, a century hence, may not improbably contain a population as large as that which now inhabits Europe. The members of her communion are certainly not fewer than a hundred and fifty millions; and it will be difficult to show that all the other Christian sects united, amount to a hundred and twenty millions. Nor do we see any sign which indicates that the term of her long dominion is approaching. She saw the commencement of all the governments, and of all the ecclesiastical establishments, that now exist in the world; and we feel no assurance that she is not destined to see the end of them all. She was great and respected before the Saxon had set foot on Britain—before the Frank had passed the Rhine—when Grecian eloquence still flourished at Antioch—when idols were still worshipped in the temple of Mecca. And she may still exist in undiminished vigour when some traveller from New Zealand shall, in the midst of a vast solitude, take his stand on a broken arch of London Bridge to sketch the ruins of St. Paul's."

There Will Always Be Love

I was still a young priest when I was faced with an agonizing moral dilemma. I had arrived the day before the wedding was to be held. The local pastor had taken care of the preliminary instructions and preparations with the couple. I was there to perform the ceremony, or more accurately, to witness their vows. Everything was ready and a spirit of joy permeated the home.

Quite by chance, the prospective bride showed me the thorough program they had prepared for the ceremony. The texts had been carefully chosen. Everything was in good order. As I absentmindedly perused the leaflet, I read the vows that they had prepared to read to each other after the manner of that time. (Couples were encouraged to write their own expression of their vows to each other in the interest of authenticity.) Some alarms went off in my head as I read their expressions of undying fidelity followed by the expression, "as long as there is love." That troubled me a bit. Surely, they did not mean to put a condition on their vows. As the evening wore on, my anxiety gnawed at my heart. It would be immoral of me to bear witness to a conditioned promise. I felt the words could be interpreted correctly. I was afraid to ask for fear I would put them in bad faith. I kept saying to myself that it was all right.

Later in the evening, alone with the father of the bride, I casually noted that I was having trouble with the expression: "as long as there is love." I rhetorically remarked that I was sure that they had not put any conditions on their vows. The father, uninitiated into the niceties of canon law, casually remarked that he wasn't too sure. Can you imagine what that did to my conscience? I slept little that night. I tossed and turned until I found a way out, short of confronting them about the exact meaning of the expression, "as long as there is love."

I handled it like this. During the homily, I called attention to the fact that the congregation would hear the couple pronounce their vows, "as long as there is love." I pointed out that the expression of vows was not just between the two, but also in the sight of God before Whom and in Whose presence they were pronouncing them. The issue was not just between two, but three, so to speak, because God is a witness. "There will always be love because God will always be there."

Only years later did the couple learn of my internal struggle on the occasion of their wedding. We have had our laughs about it. They are still happily married with a family and have not had to invoke the love of God for anything but support and strength.

Prayer: Some Personal Reflections

This essay on prayer first appeared in the St. Meinrad Newsletter, v. XIV no. 2, March 1973.

I am fascinated these days, not only by the renewed interest in prayer in all its form, but, especially, by the breadth of that interest. It is almost as if the whole Catholic people, including nuns and priests, have been zapped in some way that has obliterated all memory of experience in prayer. Every one—lay, religious, and clergy—is asking the same request Jesus once responded to: "Lord teach us to pray."

For the most part, I'm sure this interest and concern are most genuine. At times, however, I am disconcerted. Do we end up talking about it endlessly, looking for new methods, signs and the like, but never really coming to grips with praying? We gather information, probe the esoteric, list obstacles, and distinguish kinds and methods. We are like the Athenians, who were more eager to listen than respond.

To use another image, we are more like art collectors than artists. We become authorities on prayer, its nature and divisions, its history in the church and in society, but we do not try to be artists.

Some artists, it is true, have unusual perception and gifts and are able to create works of beauty without much effort, but most of them have become the artists they are by dint of hard work: practicing, testing, filling their portfolios with sketches and studies. I am suggesting that we become artists and not hobbyists, and that we be willing to work at "learning to pray"—a learning process that continues to our dying day.

Fundamental to this effort is the commitment to establishing and maintaining a deep, warm, loving relationship with God. This may be where the basic problem lies. As technology has removed much of the mystery of things and even of life, the image of a manipulating God, that is, a God who is constantly interfering in our world has yielded to a vague concept of a God totally removed. It is precisely here that our faith comes to grips with the wholly *Other*, the transcendent, incomprehensible Being whose ways are unsearchable and yet who sent His Son to teach us to think of Him as loving Father.

It seems to me that all of us, no matter where we may be in terms of closeness to God, can imitate the prayer of the man in the Gospel: "Lord, help my unbelief." This is a prayer that can be said honestly, without any feeling of phoniness, and still be confronting the very heart of the matter. When we do this, we are praying. Faith is presupposed in prayer, but it is Christian to pray for a deeper faith.

Having a time set aside means setting a value on prayer. It means setting priorities on the things we must do every day and budgeting it into our day. This very process of setting aside a time and place is a non-verbal communication already. It says to God and to ourselves that we really feel prayer is important. Writers about prayer insist there is no substitute for this. However prayerfully we may do other things, the importance—even the necessity—of this time for prayer is a primary responsibility.

As mentioned above, Jesus also told us not to use many words when we pray. We are to place ourselves quietly in God's presence; then in the language that comes to us "naturally" make our prayers. There are some basic attitudes that ought, at least at times, to be reflected in these prayers. First of all, the recognition that we are creatures and that we are dependent; that He is a Creator, totally other and yet imminent. An attitude of reverent awe before Him, or recognition that He is worthy of praise and thanks, is translated into words. After a time, even words are not necessary. Again, the words are not to tame God. They are points of contact with Him. Because of His bounteous goodness and kindness, because of His providence, we thank Him. As crazy and mixed up as our world is, who of us does not have much to be grateful for?

A step that may be missed, and frequently may be a clue to discouragement in prayer, is that reading goes hand and glove with it.

Thought starters are prayer starters. Reading is the launch pad of prayer. Off the printed page, the heart soars. At least most of the time, prayer starts with data. Data from the news, from the events of our day, from reading, especially sacred Scripture, leads to formulating our feelings in words. Formulas of words make contacts, so to speak; when contact is made and we have said our piece, silence once again is called for. It is in these moments of silence that God reads our hearts and speaks to us.

It strikes me as I write this that I am making it sound too easy. I have not forgotten how difficult it was in the beginning and still is, nor can I forget the kind of commitment to a life of prayer that I have made. These things make prayer-talk come easy and perhaps make it more real to me than it might be to others less familiar and intent on it. Even so, I believe that, under the Spirit, the Lord touches us wherever we are and draws us on. This gives zest to a life of prayer. We are constantly seeing and hearing things at different levels. One only has to consider how passages of Scripture can strike us differently at different times. Words and phrases can take on special meaning for us in the light of where we are. The same few words may deepen our awareness of our sinfulness at one time and deepen our hope in God's mercy at another; it may move us to repentance at one time and flood our souls with prayer at another.

I have mentioned the man who prayed for faith. Two other passages of the Gospel come to mind, which I like very much. The one is the scene where the blind man asks for his sight: "Lord, that I may see again." The other is the healing of the deaf man: "Ephpheta! Be opened." Both these incidents relate to a physical healing. At that level, we see Jesus responding to particular needs of individuals. Implied in both these incidents, though, is the healing of their spirits, too.

Again, wherever we may feel we are in terms of nearness to God, we can pray for spiritual healing or enrichment. "Lord, that I may see; that I may hear and understand. Help me to see beneath the surface of things. Help me to hear you and to understand what you have to say in the events of my life, in the people with whom I deal. Open my mind and heart to whatever it is you are saying to me in these moments of my life. Remove the scales from my eyes; I want to see!"

I think it is theologically sound to pray in this way. We reason that all creation is a kind of communication from God. We reason, too, and He has told us as much, that all creation speaks of His glory. One is expected to get the message and give glory to God. There are numerous historical events in which God has revealed hidden purposes. When we really believe that our provident Father sustains all things, we may rightly pray that He may reveal to us what is the meaning of any moment of our life, and how we might grow in this moment to a deeper awareness of Him so that we can respond with our whole life to the praise of His glory.

I am a librarian, and am well aware of shelf after shelf of books on prayer. What I have said can be only a sketchy personal reflection. Yet, I still hope it might stimulate someone to try a little harder. I think I can say to anyone who is willing to set aside even ten to fifteen minutes a day to making him or herself present to God in this way, that he or she will gain a clearer understanding of who they are and where they are going. I trust they will experience a deep peace and joy in life. May it be so.

Sister Marguerite Daly, I.H.M.

I wrote this at a time when there were small signs of the onset of Alzheimer's disease. I wanted Sister to be recognized when she could still enjoy the recognition. So often, we wait until someone dies to say the things we wanted to say all along. My little essay was posted in the St. Mary Convent of the Sisters of the Immaculate Conception in Monroe, MI.

On the feast of the Holy Family in this year 2000, I want to pay a special tribute to Sister Marguerite. She has already served almost 60 years in religious life. Her community has been her family these many years, but she has never forgotten her parents and her brothers. She has loved us all with a deep compassion. Further, she has shown motherly love and concern for all her nieces and nephews, and their children, not a few. It seems fitting on this feast to reflect on her many family values.

I would like to speak of her as an "angel." I have heard the sisters in her community speak of her in that way. (She was very fond of the TV program, "Touched by an Angel.") I use the term loosely, obviously. She is not incorporeal, but she sees herself as a messenger of God. The theology behind her position flows right from the Gospels and the catechism teaching about the sacraments of Baptism and Confirmation. She has a strong sense of being incorporated into Christ and open to the Holy Spirit's guidance. She has frequently spoken to me about being Christ to all she meets. Her loving unselfish openness to all has been the occasion of special graces for many. In those instances, she has been an instrument of Christ, a messenger and, in a way, an angel.

I would further like to characterize her as an angel of hospitality. The dictionary defines hospitality with three nuances: a person who is hospitable is given to generous and cordial reception of guests; is one promising or suggesting generous and cordial welcome; is one offering a pleasant or sustaining environment. Throughout her life, Sister Marguerite has modeled all of these: she has shown warm hospitality to guests; has been a most welcoming person; and, has created a pleasant and sustaining environment for the people with whom she has lived and worked.

She did those things in the many classrooms in Detroit, Trenton, Dearborn and Mobile, AL. She served as a teacher and as a librarian. I would be willing to wager that many black Americans who are successful today recall her with affection and gratitude. Indeed, some have come back to tell her so. I remember visiting her classroom at St. Boniface in Detroit. The children seemed to adore her. They attested that their happiest hours in the day were in her classroom.

At Marygrove, she took a floundering hospitality-house to new heights of charity and peace. It was there that a larger segment of her community experienced her generous heart and willing hands.

In more recent years, she had a similar position in Madonna Hall at the Convent in Monroe. There she was the hostess to many programs. Countless visitors came under her care. At the same time in these years, she reached out to the more aged and less healthy members of the community with service and affection, noted and appreciated by all.

Even in these days when she may need more help herself, she continues with inner joy and peace her thoughtful ways for others.

Sister Marguerite is also a thanksgiving person. She is grateful for her life, grateful for her faith, and especially grateful for the loving faith community with whom she seeks God in peace. Here is where she continues trying to be an instrument of Christ's love and compassion to all.

I consider it fitting that we acknowledge Sister Marguerite's gifts among us while she can enjoy the recognition. Being honored in this way will not lessen her angel-like concern and compassion for those with whom she lives and loves. May God continue to reward her here and hereafter.

Handing over the Keys to the Library

This was a little romantic idea of giving some formality to my leaving the library after 51 years. I was a little miffed that the institution did not make more of the moment.

Luba, I have asked to make an informal, formal ceremony of handing you my keys. It is a brief transaction, hand to hand. However, I would like to make a moment of it. I am not aware of any official ceremony planned by the institution, that may come, but we will make up our own.

By giving you these keys, I am entrusting to you the care and concern for the library building and its furnishings.

By turning over to you these keys, I am also highlighting the new responsibility you will bear for the collection, and the services that enhance its preservation and use. Housed here is a precious collection that tells the story from creation to the present in many ways, along with mankind's reflection on the mysteries in art, architecture and literature. Here are records of dynasties and kings, of history and culture, of science and math. Herein is a goodly record of the story of the faith community that is the church, and the faith community that is Saint Meinrad Archabbey and Seminary. Preserve what we have; enhance it as best you can.

By placing these keys in your hands, I am charging you with a leadership role in this community for things that pertain to the library. Both the monastery and the school will rely on you to lead by doing what you can with the resources you have in hand. They will rely on you for information and counsel when more funding may be required to achieve what must be done. It will not always be easy. You may have to cajole or even to fight, but I hope you will always be treated as a colleague concerned.

Finally, by turning over these keys to you, I am leaving you a loyal and dedicated staff. I trust that you will quickly discern their strengths and evoke from them a continued commitment to this worthy cause in this community. May God bless you.

Fr. Simeon

August 1, 2000

In the end, I couldn't read the last paragraph. I was crying too much. I just said, "Take the damn keys." Even romantics have their disappointments.

Old Blue Goes to College

Old Blue was a dog. This is a dog story, but it may say more about Sam and his father than it does about this extraordinary animal. You be the judge of that.

This is not my story. I heard it on the radio on Sunday, September 5, 1988, on a station out of Louisville, Kentucky. I'm not stealing the story. I just want to tell it again. The man who told it has something to do with an annual festival of storytellers in Louisville. He said it's been going on for 13 years now. The first year there were nine storytellers and six listeners. Last year there was a whole bunch of storytellers and over 10,000 listeners. There is nothing like a good story well told. I liked his "Old Blue" story. I hope you do, too.

Old Blue was a coon dog. I've never given coon hunting much thought myself, but would you believe the very next day on "Morning Edition," I learned about the coon dog cemetery in Alabama. The Tennessee Valley Coon Hunting Association maintains a cemetery where members can lay their hunting companions to rest. It is the Key Underwood Coon Dog Memorial Graveyard. No intruders allowed. A few years back, they dug up a house pet that got buried there under false pretenses. "Old Yeller," "Old Blue," "Duke," "Queen" and King" are some of the names honored there, many of them very colorful. Anyway, hearing how so many coon dogs enjoy such respect, I want to preserve the story of "Old Blue."

Near as I can, I'll tell it as I heard it, in the first person.

I grew up in Western Kentucky. Went through all the grades there in the company of a friend and classmate, Sam. Old Blue was Sam's Pa's dog. Old Blue was the pride and joy of Sam's Pa. Fact is, Sam's Pa thought more of that dog than he did of Sam. That dog had a voice like a trumpet. Even in a pack of hounds, you could always recognize his rich yowls, and knew for sure whether he was just warm, or hot on the trail. And there was nothing in the world like the sounds he made when a coon got treed. Smart, too. Wasn't nobody around that didn't credit Old Blue with being the smartest damn dog in the county.

Anyway, Sam and I were very close. We both went to the University of Kentucky together. Only ones in our class that went to college. We were taking different courses. I was in liberal arts. He was in agriculture and animal husbandry. We moved in different crowds. Sam got off on the wrong foot. He began drinking and gambling. He got deeply in debt. I couldn't help him, and was saddened to see the direction his life was taking. He didn't talk to me much about it, because he knew I disapproved.

In his distress over money, he spent hours thinking up plans for how to get more. He wrote his father saying that the university was starting a very special experimental program to teach animals to read. They need intelligent animals for the experiment. Seeing as to how Old Blue was the smartest dog around, he seemed an ideal candidate for the program. "Just send the dog and $200," he wrote, "and I'll enroll him in the program."

Well, Sam's father didn't like the idea at first. He hated to part with his dog, even for science. Then the more he thought about it, the more reasonable it seemed. Old Blue deserved the opportunity, and it wouldn't hurt his own reputation none to have a dog that could read. So he put Old Blue on the bus and sent along $200 for enrollment. Sam was delighted and hoped to win back his losses, but in no time at all he was further in debt. Stymied again, he wrote another letter to his dad.

"Thanks for sending Old Blue. You'd be right proud of how well he is doing. The faculty is very impressed. They now want to teach him to write. They say writing goes hand in hand with reading, and it would be a shame not to let Old Blue learn to write. Please send $200 for enrollment."

The money came.

And the money went. Sam was desperate, but he tried again.

"Thanks for sending the money," he said. "You wouldn't believe the progress he is making. He's the talk of the department. They are so excited. They now want me to enroll him in the experimental course for talking animals. It would be a shame to have a dog that can read and write, but not talk. Please send $200."

Sam's family was not rich. This dog was becoming a drain on their resources, but family pride in their blue ribbon coon dog won out, and $200 came in the return mail. Sam's Pa would have been shocked to know it followed after what had come before. The final ignominy was, Sam lost the dog where he had lost the money. There would have to be a reckoning, and soon. Christmas vacation was just around the corner, and we were both going home.

Sam's Pa was so excited about getting to see Old Blue again he could hardly contain himself. Naturally enough, he wanted to show off Old Blue's new learning that he had invested so much in. He called all his friends and neighbors in for the homecoming. He himself was eager to watch his dog read, write and talk. "Never heard the like," he said to himself.

Well, friends were all gathered and waiting for Sam and Old Blue when Sam pulled up in his pickup. "Git yerself in here," his father called, "and bring Old Blue." Sam just stood at the door, appalled at the assembly of admirers, eager to see Old Blue perform. Sam stayed at the door, saying he had to talk to his Pa. The old man kept calling out for him to come on in. Finally, he yielded to the lad's insistence and joined him in the pickup.

"Pa," the boy began, "I am really sorry what I have to tell you. I feel so bad about it, and I know you're going to be hurt. I've been looking forward so much to coming home! Just this morning I was in the bathroom shaving with my straight razor and I said to Old Blue, 'Old Blue, I can hardly wait to get home and see my folks again. It's been so long we've been away.' Old Blue was sitting there reading the paper. He said, 'Me too.' Then after a moment, he added, 'I especially miss your Pa. He's been so good to me.' Then he hesitated a moment before he went on to say: 'Also I'm wondering if he is still carrying on with that young school teacher.'

"Pa, I don't know what got into me, but I lit out after that dog and slit his throat then and there. I killed him before I knew it. I was so upset. And now I don't hardly know what to say."

There was a long pause. The old man swallowed a couple of times, put his arm around Sam and said, "You done the right thing, son, you done the right thing."

The Bells of Saint Meinrad

This little essay appeared in a Saint Meinrad newsletter in the mid-seventies. I was asked to write it to stimulate interest in acquiring and replacing bells. As such, it was very much of a period piece. I have omitted the paragraph asking for bells. The rest is pretty much the way it appeared in the newsletter.

Recently, I read what I thought was a delightful essay on bells. This has prompted me to want to talk a bit about our bells, because I suspect that most of the alumni and friends of Saint. Meinrad have a warm feeling for them. I certainly do. At the moment, big number six is cracked and so it cannot be struck. The mechanism on the tower clock is out of whack. I, for one, hope something can be done to replace the one and repair the other so that the regular round of sounds will once more be a part of our day. Anyway, it won't hurt to talk about them.

As a young student, I had to memorize Poe's "Bells," and deliver it in elocution class. Some of those rhymes and sounds still rattle around my head. They were my first serious introduction to something I have come to enjoy so much—making phrases with colorful sounds and musing on things fragmentedly. Bear with the snippets of thought and sound I intersperse here about bells. Quite frankly, I lack the time and skill to round them into finished pieces. They are the whimsy of one who wishes he could do more.

> *Morning bells—a pulse of rich sound pounding on the window-pane,*
> *Calling all to bless Him at the beginning of the day.*

Three times in particular, bells have had a special meaning for me. The thanksgiving bells that announced the end of World War II will always stand out in my memory. Abbot Ignatius had advised all departments that whenever the declaration was announced, the bells should be rung solemnly for 15 minutes. All the monks and students in the meantime should gather in the church to sing the *Te Deum.* How exhilarating were the joyful and cheering sounds when eventually the bells pealed out the good news.

> *Vesper bells—ribbons of rhythm floating down on a sleepy*
> *Village, marking the end of another day of praise.*

It is such a passing thing, but I put a lot of emphasis on our "wedding" bells as monks. The evening before Solemn Vows, after Vespers, and again in the morning, it is a custom to ring all six of our bells to announce the celebration. Even though we were on retreat then, my classmates gathered in a room the night before our Solemn Vows to listen and rejoice together at the joyous sounds. It is hard to believe the big number six has already tolled its death knell for two of them. (More have died since.)

> *Healthy bells tell whatever they are told to.*
> *They toll too, but only when the news is bad.*
> *Had it been good, they'd ring and sing.*
> *Noting only in passing the passing hours of an ordinary dingdong day.*

The other special memory I have was also a toll. I was napping when the big bell boomed out on November 22, 1963. It was the beginning of an orgy of sorrow many of us will never forget—the death and burial of President John F. Kennedy.

It is just such things as these that have made bells an intimate part of the lives of individuals and the history of communities down through the ages. Actually, mankind seems to have had them as a part of life already by the time humans come out the shadows and appear on the horizon of what we call history. Bells provided rhythms for dances, "protection" from threatening spirits, and rich sounds for celebrations.

It is not likely that the Christian church used them before the Edict of Milan in 313. The very early Christian churches were built without towers for bells, but in the Middle Ages—at least by 1000 A.D.—the tower with bells was an integral part of every church. The bells were used not only to signal hours of worship but also to announce many other occasions, such as death, fire, or festival.

The bells of the tower clock call out each quarter hour.
They tame time,
Rolling it into segments of sixty divided by four.
Twenty-four little circles with four arcs of fifteen
Instead of one relentless line of one thousand four hundred and forty minutes.
Who could take it?

The "passing" bell was rung to call for prayers for someone who was dying. It was a toll that ended in a burst of ringing when the person died, to celebrate his passing out of the valley of tears. This double kind of ringing is preserved in the toll as used now, here and elsewhere, except these ringings are done only after the person has died. The number of years the monk has been professed determines the number of tolls.

Bells have tongues, but speak no evil.
They cry, but have no eye.
Bells can express sorrow, but can't give sympathy.
The bell-ringer can do both.

Because they are so intimately connected with worship, bells are consecrated. An elaborate ritual is prescribed to initiate these material things into the realm of the sacred. Perhaps, the great emphasis here stemmed from the fact that bells were also used for worship by pagans. There was much superstition over the power of bells to tame evil spirits. Certainly of importance here is the whole theology of blessing anything a Christian uses as a part of the restoration of all things in Christ, wresting all creation by blessing and consecration from the dominion of the devil. In some early Pontificals, the consecration of bells was similar to the rite of Baptism with baptismal robes and sponsors—the whole thing.

Since I have been at Saint Meinrad, we have consecrated only two bells. Number 5 had cracked and was replaced. [Number 6 was replaced in connection with the renovation of the church in 1996. The blessing took place right in front of the entry doors of the monastery before it was hoisted to its place in the tower.]

Bells are not for introverts.
They are not good for secrets either.
They are mostly good for people.
For people who have some message to tell, or feeling to share.
They're dead give-away that live people are around,
At least, someone to ring them and someone for whom they are rung.

The very earliest model of the Abbey, based on a drawing by one of the founding Fathers, shows a bell outside the house. Between 1854 and 1959, a bell was hung from a nearby willow tree. In 1859, three bells were bought by Fr. Ulrich Christen. These bells were given to local parishes when in 1885 six new bells were purchased. These bells were victims of the fire in 1887, but the same metal was used to remold the set that were mounted in the towers of the Abbey Church when it was rebuilt from 1899-1904. These are the bells that have marked the joys and sorrows, the comings and goings of this community: professions, ordinations, funerals, wars, blessings of abbots, visits by prelates (such as Cardinal Ritter, Archbishop Cicognanni, apostolic delegate to USA, Abbot Primates), Fatima Week, rogation days, Corpus Christi processions and all the other celebrations that are the warp and woof of this faith community nestled here in the hills.

There's a kind of mystical communication between the bell-ringer and the bell.
They are in an intimate relationship, yet never see each other.
The bell rope is the ringer's only contact.
Yet by steady pull and release he makes the bell call out like a talking puppet.
After a while it's hard to tell
Whether the pull of the ringer sounds the bell,
Or the sound of the bell makes the ringer pull.

Now the bells ring. They ring when someone is tugging on the rope that leads high into the tower. Occasionally, a suggestion is made that this all too primitive and nobody rings bells anymore, and that it is hard work, and tedious, and an electronic system would sound better anyway. So far, we have been able to see beyond the toil and tedium to the rich communication that takes place when young men of faith gather in a tower and pull ropes that peal out a gladsome sound, telling all the world that God is near, and men are here to praise Him.

Dearest Angel

I am not quite sure how to tell the story of David Singer. That I remember his name is some indication that I must have made special note of it. He was a friend of Mother. First, let me say a word about Mother.

As a girl, Mother was petite, weighing only 98 pounds at the time of her marriage in 1915. She was very active, vivacious, and outgoing. She loved to dance.

David came into her life while she was still in high school. They did not date, but they were in the same group that did a lot of recreating and partying together. David was smitten. The relationship was doomed from the start, though, because he was not a Catholic. As much as it may have hurt her, for her, there were no options. He faded from her life.

However, on any number of occasions, Mother would speak of him. We children always wonder what this mysterious fellow must have been like. We were a little taken aback one evening when a car pulled out front, and a short, roly-poly, bald man came up the steps. He knew the house from his youth and wondered if Marguerite might possibly live here. I was a teenager at the time and was quite excited when he said that he was David Singer. I doubt if my Father had ever met him. I presume David was gone from the scene before Dad showed up. Dad knew the name, though, and I was quite chagrined that he did not receive him more warmly. It so happened that Mother was quite ill at the time and was up in bed. I was ready to take him upstairs, but my Father never gave the invitation. We stood around on the porch for a while. He left without seeing Mother. At that time, it had probably been 30 years since they had seen each other.

After Dad had died, David must have heard that Mother was in a nursing home; by then she was around 75 years old. Wouldn't you know, he came out to visit her on several occasions, and he wrote her sweet notes, addressing her as Dearest Angel. Well, at the time, Mother had all her faculties, but she was anything but a romantic figure, probably tipping the scales over 200 pounds. When I would have an opportunity to visit, she would show me his notes and speak glowingly of his sweetness. He was close to 80 years old. I learned more about him. He lived in Lexington, Kentucky. He had been on the faculty of the University of Kentucky for most of his career, teaching automotive engineering.

It so happened that I had business in Lexington and I made it a point to visit him. It was absolutely delightful. He had been involved in cars all his life and had a classic vintage auto, which he drove to exhibitions as opportunity provided. His trips to Detroit were in his big car and it was in that behemoth that he drove out to Pontiac to visit Mother.

We had a most pleasant visit. His wife of all these years was pleasant, but a bit reserved around the Roman collar and did not sit in on our conversation while he described his young affection for Mother. He told me he was working in Detroit for some auto company at the time, c. 1912, and he borrowed a car to drive from Detroit to Monroe just to ride around the campus where Mother was in school, in hopes of seeing her. He didn't. While now the trip is an easy 30-minute drive, when he drove it he sometimes plowed through fields and marshes. There were no roads for cars at the time. Anyway, we had a delightful conversation and I left aglow at the vivacity of the old man who still remembered with affection his dearest angel.

I never saw him again. I was so grateful to have met him, though, and I thought I had a little better insight into the private life of my Mother, the toothless little bundle of fat confined to a wheelchair, who could still love and be loved in delicate ways.

Reflection on a Pinecone

This essay was written for a workshop for faculty on writing.

A craggy, crusty piece of woody growth, a pinecone, colorless, misshapen, ugly, stands, for all that, as a rich symbol of life and hope. More is to come. Much has gone before. What all has gone into its shaping? What will it become?

I remember a little orphan boy I met one time. He was dirty and unkempt. He had been mistreated and abused, but there was something in the clarity of his eyes and the freshness of his smile that gave hope and promise for the time to come. Funny, how a grotesque seed can bring so much to mind.

A biologist could put this pinecone in its place, classify it, fit it into the scheme of things. I would rather marvel at the mystery of life and death in the nature of things. This one cone symbolizes all that has gone before and all that will come after. Locked in its cells is the power to become a mighty tree. How awesome that the simplest things of life continue to give and grow and give again.

The ecology of our planet has made this possible. Are we about to snuff out this cycle by the carelessness of our ways? Is this, perhaps, the last season for pinecones?

A Reflection after a Storm at Sea

Jan. 16th, 1968. At sea. I have just come in from the deck where I have stood for some time watching an orgy of sorts. The elements are all charged up and making quite a ruckus. There is something kind of primordial about it. The winds do not plow as men do, making a trough along the path they tread, but rather push the troughs toward some distant shore where they will be beat out level again.

There is this thing about the sea. It resents us. This monster ship upon its surface is catalyst—an emetic of sorts—that creates a great rejecting turbulence. It all seems so fruitless—such a waste of energy. Is the sea so stupid that it has not learned to live with progress? Must it go through these tantrums every time? Or will there come a day when it will welcome us? I know not, but I take a kind of pleasure watching the struggle take place, like watching a street fight where the bully gets done in.

It really is something awesome, this brutal display of nature. One cannot help but be aware he is observing one of the basic elements or two as wind and water join forces.

The constant motion over its surface is generative, in fact. Is not all life traceable to the sea? For centuries of centuries, the mating process has gone on. Sometimes peacefully. Sometimes violently as now. But it goes on.

We pass over its surface, adapt ourselves to its mood, and pass by unaware of the underlying processes, creative and destructive, that are here and now at work.

As aware as I am of my inability to comprehend it all, I am deeply grateful for this opportunity to be confronted with raw nature in this way. Even if it is from the relative safety and comfort of this ship.

Not unrelated to these thoughts of beginnings and endings are my sentiments now as I realize a very important interlude of my life is coming to an end. Each moment we move from East to West, the end of an unbelievably lovely time in my life draws near. This is not a despairing thought. It's a moody one. I go back to a life I have chosen and I choose once more. I have no regrets with this destiny of my life, but I cannot shake this brooding. I do not try. It pleases me.

As surely as a phase of my life is coming to an end, may I not look at it as the beginning of a new one, with new hopes, new adventures to come? I think of it this way when I see the anxiety and tension on the faces of young people on the boat who are leaving home and country to start a new life in the states. Tomorrow a new day will dawn. Whether the sun shines on us, or whether it will be a cold, snowy and sleety day like now, I hope it will be for all of us, a day of confident expectancy, and but the beginning of years of fruitful accomplishment in peace.

The Stranger

This is a true story by John Daly, a nephew, as told to me in July 1985.

The rain earlier that day had cleared the air. Everything took on a radiance and sharpness that uplifted my spirit. The sun was low in the sky, but still strong enough to bring out the brilliance of the trees and the flowers as I headed down the highway for home. I was in an expansive mood.

I began to reflect on my life and its goals as I sped along the interstate. At 25, a Midwesterner, I was in a fast lane in the East. I mused over what was happening. My business skills were sharpening. I was moving up the corporate ladder, slowly but surely. I was being challenged at every step and loved it. My mind seldom wavered from the concerns of my business life. Not out of any weakness, I allowed myself some questions about where my heart was, about whether I was becoming hardened, self-centered and cold. Was the very realizing of some of my goals stifling others that had been instilled in me from my youth?

Perhaps had I not been absorbed in this vein, I would not have gotten off the highway at the wrong exit. Perhaps I would not have been on the side road where I could see this old man in a white suit stumbling and then slowly collapse in a heap in a field to my right. Almost instinctively, I turned at the next corner and circled back. Now when I think of it, I wonder about my lack of hesitation. I didn't, though. Hesitate, I mean. In no time at all, I was at his side. I remember how my tie dangled down as I leaned over him and asked if he needed help. He looked up at me in a rather dazed way and then his eyes filled up and he began to sob.

The story came out only gradually. I had only been there a few moments when a police officer came by to see what the trouble was. He gave the old man directions on how to get to the local bus station so he could get to his hometown. He was too drunk to comprehend, but the officer didn't seem to notice. The little town where he said he lived was not far out of the way for me. I volunteered to drive him home.

Drunks can be effusively grateful. Something else was going on here, though. My new friend's wife had recently died. He had been devastated, but had managed to get through the wake and funeral without incident. Now, some weeks later, he had bussed to this nearby town to clean up some business and visit a friend. With the support of his wife, he had not touched alcohol in 18 years. Today, his unsuspecting friend insisted he have a few drinks. The remorse at falling off his program was almost as debilitating as the alcohol itself. He constantly fought back tears as he poured out his story.

I got him home. A small bungalow it was. Even to me, it felt empty without his wife, and I easily sensed how empty and lonesome he was feeling. As I stood to leave, I reached out to him and put my arms around him. He shook with sobs as I held him for a brief moment. Then he looked at me through his tears, wistfully, and told me that that was the first time he had been embraced by a man since the graduation of his son some 30 years before. It was an awkward moment, but I got the message of how deeply grateful he was for my kindness. He assured me he would be all right now, as he more soberly, but nonetheless effusively, expressed his appreciation.

I left him standing there on the lawn of his home, waving to a stranger who, in the course of a few short hours, had touched him deeply. And I, as I drove away, was grateful that I had been that stranger.

July 5, 1985

Door of My Cell

I moved into my cell in the old monastery August 6, 1951, the same day I began to be the head librarian. Fr. Placidus, my predecessor in the library, had lived in that room, which was also the Prior's office for a good number of years. Over the years, I had posted signs on the door three times. I like the thoughts behind them.

+

Pax

For 25 years this door
Has opened and closed for me;
Has welcomed my comings and goings.

For 25 years these walls have
Harbored the sorrows and
Joys of a passing life.

For these years and the more than double that
That went before,
I salute you.

—August 16, 1976.

+

Pax

For 30 years this door and this room
Have been a shelter and shield.
The comings and goings of half a lifetime
Have been witnessed here.

A haven, a harbor for me
Day after day,
And for how many before me since 1888.

I salute with gratitude
This door and this cell.
Numbered are the days
It can so continue to serve.

—August 16, 1981

+

Pax

Farewell
From one who leaves this place,
Knowing full well,
No other space will so long serve his needs
Before he's gone.

Since August 16, 1951,
You have harbored one
Not kind to your face,
But who loved this place
Where you sheltered his comings and goings.

Thank you!
Fond adieu,
Sweet door!
Nevermore will you welcome or hide
This one who is grateful for the shade
You have so long provided.

—July 1982

It nevermore housed a single soul. It was razed with the rest of the building about 1987.

St. John the Baptist

✦

Homily given June 24, 2001, for the
Benedictine Sisters of Bristow, VA.

St. John the Baptist is one of whom Jesus said there was no greater prophet. He was the forerunner, the one who was designated to announce specifically the coming of the Messiah, the Redeemer of the world, the Savior of God's people.

Like Mary, we know very little about him. Because of his important role, Luke's Gospel shows many parallels between his birth and Jesus'. Both have a special communication, the story of the birth, the circumcision and naming of the chiild. Mary has a canticle at the time of the visitation to Elizabeth, already carrying in her womb the Child promised her; Zachary proclaims his when he names John, the first words he had spoken in nine months. Our Gospel this morning highlights the naming of John, and the canticle of Zachary.

John's ministry was fruitful. He preached the coming of the kingdom, the need for a complete change of heart to be open to that great mystery. It was his role to announce Jesus' presence, to point Him out as the Lamb of God, long awaited by the Jewish people.

A surely painful, but grace-filled moment in John's life is when he remarked: "He must increase, and I must decrease." John had a role to play. He did his job, and in doing it acquired great notoriety. Crowds flocked to see and hear him. Now that Jesus had come, it was John's role to fade out of the picture. I would like to suggest that John pointed out a very important principle that each of us can use in our own spiritual journey. "He must increase, and I must decrease."

It doesn't take long for anyone engaging, seriously, in the spiritual life to become aware, sometimes painfully, of how selfish and self-centered we are. This little formula is a handy mantra for getting ourselves in line. Jesus' love and compassion, gentleness and self-control are to increase in us, at the expense of all those small and selfish ways of our small hearts. To be more Christ-like in our relations with one another, we need to let go of our petty needs and smallness of heart.

St. John, by your prayers and example, help us to learn to let the virtues of Christ increase in our daily lives. "He must increase, and I must decrease!"

Tom, a Man with a Vision

Katie's father, Obie, owned an insurance agency. Both Katie and Tom worked for him. Early in their married lives, they began to assess what their future was in the company. They saw little hope of ever being major owners. After due deliberation and with the approval of Obie, they decided that Tom should launch out on his own. It was scary for the first few years. There were few clients. Living and office expenses ate up what little profit there was.

I think it was after the first year of being on his own, Tom wrote to me expressing his concern for the lack of profits. He said he sat around his small office often with little to do but wait and hope.

I remember I sent back a rather sharply worded note urging him to get out of his chair and cultivate other business opportunities from his office, such as filing tax reports for customers and possibly selling real estate, as had been done in the other office.

I got back from him a rather touching letter thanking me for my counsel, but offering an explanation for not following it. He said that he really believed in the importance of insurance for individuals and families. Although he hoped to make a living doing it, he did not feel he had to con anyone. What he was selling was essential to any good family financial plan. He was very comfortable with his role. He said he wanted to be the best insurance agent he could be. Therefore, he did not want to clutter up his interest and time with other distracting processes. He had seen enough in the other office to know that, during tax time or in periods given over to real estate, insurance was less attended to. He felt it may take him a while but he preferred to stay with his specialty. His vision and his forthrightness humbled me. I believe that his attitude helped him to be the success that he was in insurance.

I would also like to note that Katie and Tom made all their major decisions as a team. Any major issue, and specifically one of financial concern, was thoroughly aired out together. I think I can safely say that Tom never made a major move or shift without the approval of Katie. If the issues were complicated, Katie was brought up to speed so she could help make an intelligent decision.

A touching proof of that was witnessed by the whole family on the occasion of their turning over some stock to each of the grandchildren. When Tom got caught up in the emotions of this generous gift, and couldn't go on, Katie calmly stood up and explained in considerable detail the nature of the transfer and its implications. It was a beautiful moment all around!

Fr. Simeon
April 15, 2001

Wedding Reflection for Loretta and Marty

This was a homily for the wedding of Loretta and Martin Daly, a nephew, on July 12, 1987.

Today, Loretta and Marty, is the first day of the rest of your lives. As trite as that may sound, I say it to emphasize—even to celebrate—this new beginning you make today. How many of us wish we could begin again and to do it right this time. How exciting and inspiring your willingness to make a fresh start, putting aside some old cares, taking up new responsibilities for one another. This is the first day.

How fitting that on this first day of your commitment to each other that you come to this place, to this sacred space, and prayerfully thank God for His blessings in your lives and ask that God to bless your love for one another. The union you pledge before your Lord is destined to be a small sign of God's love for us. Your fidelity and persevering love is an echo for all of us to hear. Your fidelity and persevering love writes large for the rest of us to see and be reminded of that faithful and eternal love that God has shown for us. We begin your life together in the presence of the God of love, before whom you pledge your troth. How fitting, indeed!

Our society pays loud lip service to the values of fidelity and family and persevering love. The undercurrent—the push and pull of daily life is quite other. Separation, divorce, infidelity and deceit are glamorized on every side. I need not dwell on these realities. I bring them up at all simply as a fair warning to you that the path you are planning for yourselves today will face many obstacles. Maintaining your stated values will mean you must move against the current. I ask you and the rest of your family and friends gathered round you to encourage you to set your values high, and then follow them out with courage. The going will not be easy, but you can do it. You have the example of a host of family and friends who have been loyal and faithful. Follow them and do not be deceived by the double standards with glamorous undercurrents so blatantly displayed by our society.

Prayer is not just asking for something from God. Before anything else prayer—any prayer—admits your dependence on God. Recognize that dependence; do not hesitate to call God's attention to that dependence. From it, your need for help flows. Thanking and glorifying your Creator come first. Being a prayerful couple is a value of the first order. Let humble prayer be a fundamental part of your lives.

Be unique. Treasure your individuality, but channel it toward the unity that you espouse today. Foster what unites and makes for peace. Shun selfishness and be quick to root out what leads to disunity and a lack of peace.

Much more, obviously, could be said. Advice is easy to give. In the long run, it is only seasoning. The quality of your love and the life you will live together are the substance, and only you can manage that.

My hope is that the beauty of this day and the intensity of this hour will be a constant reminder to you through the years of the importance of the work you take up today. Prayer, music, candles, the presence of loved ones and friends, all of these combine to impress you deeply with the importance of this work you begin together. We support you and encourage you. Our prayer is that the solemnity of this hour will continue to support you and spur you on in the ever-deepening process of being family.

Today is the first day of the rest of your lives.

Some Reflections on the Writing Process

This essay was written for a workshop for faculty on writing.

I empathize with those who struggle to revise an original piece of writing. Frequently, my revised text says something entirely different from the first draft, because I recognize some illogical progression, or a leap that I have made in my thinking. The text is evidence of a lack of clarity of thought in the first draft.

I am also intrigued by the concept of multi-levels in writing. Sometimes consciously, often unconsciously, I develop lines of thought that are open to communicating at different levels. Since most of my writing is on a religious topic or for the purpose of motivating, I believe I use words and phrases that can be "heard" at different levels. I hear myself as a teacher at one level and as a practitioner at another. I can almost detect on second or third reading where I have moved from a theorist expressing teachings I have been given to the person who has experienced and lived a truth he wishes to share. A subtle shift, but it is there—in the words—in the timbre of the voice when the words are spoken.

I am an avid reader. I enjoy stories. I am easily awed by the skills of authors who weave patterns of words that awaken feelings and images and sounds in my head and heart. I sometimes cry out at the beauty of a passage that moves me. I am sometimes so moved that I literally leave my reading place to collar someone with whom I can share my find—a practice, even when indulged in rarely, that does not endear one even to friends.

I remember once, in the process of cataloging Newman's sermons, I was deeply touched by his sermon on the "Parting of Friends." I was so moved by the final paragraph or so that I interrupted the work of Miss Skinner, our head cataloger. I read the passage aloud with tears in my eyes and a cracking voice. I had not taken into consideration that she was a devout Anglican. I realized how insensitive I had been when into the silence came the rhythmic click clack of her typewriter. I was too stunned to apologize. We never ever spoke of it again.

As a librarian, I am able, on occasion, though the occasions become rarer as I become more ossified in administrative duties, to awaken in others an enthusiasm for the word. (Word here is multileveled symbol. It could mean literature, a good book, an accurate reference, Scripture, or the Son of God.) I am not a teacher in the classroom, but I am not without resources when dealing with a student, one on one. I am glad I am an avid reader, and enjoy being a librarian.

I also write. Not a lot, but I write enough to know the agony and the ecstasy of the process. I know firsthand—with a pen in it—the difficulties the writer faces as he or she sits poised before the blank sheet. No time now to become someone else with other skills. Now is the hour and I must go with what I have. The whole history and mystery of who I am, how I analyze, how I make judgments, is on the line here. The fantastic process takes place in me from head and heart to hand and pen. Soon, through the medium of a few marks on a page, I will be able to reach out to another's mind and heart so that what is going on in me can go on in him or her. How dependent I am in those moments on skills learned over years of practice. Yes, I am a librarian and not a teacher. When I write, though, I think of myself as a teacher without benefit of podium.

Another Version of Day One

The first time I saw the Abbey towers, we were coming from the east on old State Road 62. We were glued to the windows of our Model A Ford as we followed the curvy way. My mother broke the silent awe we all felt. "This is one telephone call I am not going to make," she said. The announcement came out of the blue. We knew what she meant, because we had been instructed to call the porter as soon as we arrived at the seminary lobby.

"Well, I am not going to make it," my father said under his breath. My brother and I both said something similar. A heavy silence fell over us as we moved through town that day in early September 1936. Nobody seemed willing to take the initiative. The original announcement was very uncharacteristic of my mother, who never met a stranger and seemed at ease in all situations. The rest of us were more backward and our responses were what one might have expected.

After we had come up the winding hill with small cedars planted along the way on either side and parked the car on the gravel between the trees, all four of us entered the barely furnished lobby and proceeded to stare at the phone. For several tense moments, no one budged. What the men had in their favor in this auspicious moment was that Mother absolutely had to find a restroom. She eventually made the call to get the instructions she needed. Shortly after, Fr. Aemelian Elpers greeted us and made us welcome.

We spent the night in the Wonderland Inn down town. Very early the next morning, they left me on the campus to wait for the arrival of Fr. Aemelian. They could not wait because they needed to get back to Michigan so Dad could go to work. I waved them good-bye as they drove off.

I was very much alone sitting on a bench wondering what was going to become of me. I was 14 years old, 430 miles from home, in a state I had never put my foot in until now. I did not know a soul, except Fr. Aemelian, whom I had met the day before. It was kind of scary. I was scared, but also excited about what may lay ahead. Now over 60 years later, I am a little awed by this recollection. I never turned back.

Formula for Growing Old Gracefully

Love, intellectual pursuits
and exercise
Are ways to counter
The passing years.

Mind, heart and body
Are thus toned,
And time's toll tempered.

—November 7, 1982

Mary Waited, an Advent Homily

Mary waited. Trained in the Scriptures Mary longed for the coming of the Messiah. She knew the hopeful message Isaiah had promised. Her heart was ready as she pondered these things, little dreaming of the role she was to play. Waiting, for her, was not standing at the door, or watching the roadway. Her waiting and watching were in the disposition of her heart, as she did the simple things required of her as a young religious woman of her time. She knew the Scriptures. Mary waited.

"Be it done unto me according to your word," was the ready response of a disciplined disciple of the living God, when God's will was made known to her. Her "how can this be?" was not a protest of doubt, nor of hesitation, but a call for clarification. Her humility, her openness to God's will was a far cry from David's haughtiness in the first reading as he attributed to himself the reign of peace his country enjoyed. He had to be made mindful that God was the true king of Israel. No rebuke was needed for Mary. She waited. She listened. And she said, "Be it done unto me according to your word."

The world will never be the same again. How awesome the moment. How the principalities and powers must have been frozen in their tracks as they awaited the response of a simple Jewish maiden that, for all time, would change the course of history. With those few simple words spoken, the heavens opened and the clouds rained down the Son of Justice. The Word of God leaped down from His throne on high and, through the narrow channel of the womb of the virgin, entered into our world. Entered into our lives, transforming hope into destiny. "Be it done unto me according to thy word." The world will never be the same again.

Our Advent season has disposed us to wait, to watch and to listen. We watched and listened to Isaiah; we watched and listened to John the Baptist; we watched and listened to Mary. Each has been a model, each offered insight into the dispositions we need to be prepared for the advent of our God. We ritualize His coming in the coming Christmas season. Symbol it is. All symbol of the transforming, healing coming of the loving God into the lives and hearts of each of us. How appropriate is our waiting, our openness, our ongoing expectation of the advent of the Christ in this advent season.

As truly as the word was made flesh in the womb of Mary, the word comes into our gifts. Simple bread, simple wine—signs of our *fiat*—let it be done unto me...are transformed into lifegiving nourishment for our souls. Food for the way. Support for the journey. Christmas on Friday is but the sign of God's coming into our lives today.

Flag Day, 1992

This was written for our newsletter celebrating the painted flagpole and the generosity of Br. Lambert.

June 14 is Flag Day this year. No big deal around here, but it was a little special this year. Old Glory was unfurled and snapping in the wind with particular grace and beauty. Until now, the flag had not been raised for months. The pole had been struck by lightening and its whole upper works destroyed. Its repair in time for Memorial Day and Flag Day was an occasion for joy in the community. The pole had been repainted top to bottom and a new flag had been purchased. The stars and stripes were a particularly beautiful sight this year on Flag Day.

Who cares for the flag? No one is assigned, as they were for the first few years after the flagpole was dedicated with pomp and circumstance back in the early '40s. In those war days, the flag was raised with trumpet and cannon blast, and lowered with "Taps." For the past 30 years, Br. Lambert has been the unappointed, unofficial, unassuming custodian who has practiced his deep sense of patriotism with his hands and feet. No speech. No fanfare. No recognition or reward. He just does it. Nike has captured the expression, "Just do it," but Br. Lambert had put meaning into the expression before Nike was around.

Who cares for the flag? Br. Lambert does. Who puts up and takes it down on Sundays, holidays and feasts? Br. Lambert does. Who was most happy on Flag Day when the breeze flapped the huge symbol of our country and our freedoms on a newly painted 100-foot pole? That's easy. Br. Lambert was. Thank you, Br. Lambert.

Mail Management

This little piece of whimsy was handwritten to a lady I knew only through correspondence. She later left the Carmel community at Terre Haute. I had made a carbon of my letter and saved it. I share it because it may say something about me, but it is also a nice description of a moment.

November 3, 1978

Dear Sister Judith,

Over the years, I have enjoyed a way of dealing with correspondence that has worked out rather well for me. When mail comes that needs immediate attention, I usually manage to deal with it. If it is a completed transaction requiring no more attention, I throw it away. If, for some reason, I want to get back to it, but not immediately, I leave it on my desk.

There it rides the tides, sometime surfacing for a few days like flotsam, only to be swamped again, disappearing for perhaps months at a time. Some letters have floated up and down on this sea of papers for years. They become familiar. Each time they reappear, a mental correspondence takes place that is a communion of souls in a way, even though my correspondent is totally unaware of our conversation.

I am in a nervous panic at the moment because a trusty helper here—a woman of indomitable will—has declared war on my "system." I must have a clean, clear-top desk so that I can be seen behind it, so that there is space to write, so that something may be placed upon it without half of last month's business crashing to the floor. She has a point and I am trying to cooperate. She sees my holding on to notes as some sort of vanity, a way of holding on to passing moments of warmth, as some miser with his shekels. And she is right.

All this by way of saying your note of April 21, which you will scarcely remember, has been with me here these many days. What you wrote in passing I have reread these 20 times and more. The friendly brown card, so familiar to me now, appears and says hello and then repeats your message of friendship. For a brief moment, I reflect on how I might respond to your kind offer of prayers and kindness.

Thus blessed, I return to everyday affairs and the brown card gets covered or floats off to another corner of the desk to await its next opportunity to speak to me.

I think you see why I dread this new regimen that offers no reruns, no nudges of sweet recall. I'll never make it. I'll die of efficiency. I'll starve from undernourished affection. I'll cheat. I know I will. Or else I must insist my friends be more frequent with their infrequent notes—a burden I do not wish to place on them.

Adieu, adieu fond note from Judith. I'll miss your comings and goings the more that no other is here to take you place.

Now, Sister, excuse this whimsy. I have so enjoyed pouring out these meandering thoughts, which though playful, carry much truth about my vanities. I enjoy squeezing out meanings in small realities and I find my use of mail an interesting little bit of psychological reinforcement, over and above the inefficiency of not being able to finish business and be done with it. I have always envied those who do loads of business but have a clear desk. My room, where said lady holds no sway, is a scandalous mound of Simeonana—a veritable junk pile that must be cleaned out.

Do pray for me, Sister, for singleness of heart, for vision, for perseverance, and for that kind of love for God and people and things that Jesus asks of us.

In His name,

Simeon

Christmas in the Monastery

I was asked to write this for possible use in a newsletter about 2002. I am not sure it ever was used.

Christmas in the monastery is not the same as Christmas at home. The painful process, for a young monk, of being weaned away from the warmth of family, home and hearth, is most deeply felt at Christmastime. Some of the measures the community takes ease the break, but none of them quite fills the gap. For instance, there are almost always a few boxes under the tree in the calefactory for novices and junior monks. These gifts are more symbol than substance, usually a more playful than practical gift. Opening them, though, in informal settings, brings a nice feel of camaraderie, and helps to supply new "family ties" for the beginners.

"Gloria in excelsis Deo et in terra pax hominibus bonae voluntatis." The rich, melodious four-part harmony of the "Angel's Song" has echoed through the silent monastery corridors with joy on Christmas Eve for over 100 years. A number of the monks consider this one of the most memorable moments of Christmas at Saint Meinrad. It is the signal that begins the Christmas celebrations. No one knows exactly when the custom began. Perhaps the custom and the music came from Einsiedeln. The story is told that all the music was lost in the great fire of September 2, 1887, and that Fr. Thomas Meier, O.S.B., a young musician of the Abbey, wrote out the parts from memory. For many years, the "angels" were anonymous. The four of them moved from floor to floor in the old monastery in cucullas and with their hoods drawn up over their heads. In more recent years, a group of 12 to 16 make their various stops, beginning at the door of Fr. Archabbot. The hushed group scurries from floor to floor, ending up in the calefactory in front of the fireplace. A number of monks, already up and ready to go, wait there for the joyful announcement. The schola then moves to the church, where a goodly number of the faithful from the surrounding area and beyond have already gathered, "Let the celebrations begin," they seem to say. "Christ is born. Gloria in excelsis Deo."

Midnight Mass, in keeping with a long-standing custom of the Roman Church, is an occasion of special celebration. The archabbot is the principal celebrant. It is the concluding moment to the long preparations of the Advent season. For the monks who carefully observe the rites of the liturgical year, Christmas is a pivotal moment between the Old and the New Testament. Before Vatican II, the ceremonies were rather elaborate, with over 30 participating in the sanctuary. For a period in the late 1940s and early 1950s, WHAS, a radio station in Louisville, KY, broadcast the Mass live. Fr. Rupert remembers with particular pleasure the tense atmosphere after all was in readiness; the whole congregation waited for the stroke of midnight when the intonation of the first words of the Introit, "Dixit Dominus Domino Meo," filled the church with song.

The scheduled services, Masses and Liturgy of the Hours, are the official monastic celebrations, governed by official bulletin-board signs from the superiors. Many other events take place because of the generosity of the brethren. It is almost all volunteer work. The house prefect, the Refectorian, the Sacristan may post signs requesting volunteers to help in the decoration of the House, the dining room, and the church. Chopping trees and delivering them is a major project. Trees are placed in the church, in the lobby of the monastery, in the calefactory, and in the refectory. Decorating the trees becomes a community activity of sorts. All this preparation gets done in the short span of a few days before Christmas.

The community has tried manfully to resist the erosion of the Advent spirit so prevalent in our culture. In recent years, one evening is devoted to decorating the tree in the calefactory. Hot chocolate is served and an effort is made to involve as many of the community as possible in trimming the tree. This promotes a familial atmosphere and nurtures the sense of community that Br. Marmion speaks of when asked what stands out in his mind about our celebration of Christmas. "I would have to say the spirit and fellowship that exists within the community during this time."

Fr. Raymond has been stationed at Catholic University for some years, but he always returns for special community celebrations, including Christmas. He says, "Once I get back, of course, I usually help with the decorating and things like that." For a number of years now, he and a couple of cohorts have taken on the responsibility for decorating the tree in the refectory. When asked why he does that, he says: "It is a matter of entering into the spirit of the feast and the time. Of course, the liturgy, the communal prayer helps tremendously with that. Even the efforts at decorating help to realize the richness that we have in and through Christ, through what the meaning of Christmas is about, God's love for humanity. I really get into the spirit of gratitude and gratefulness to God, and to the community with which I feel very connected and supported."

Christmas cards are made available to the monks as needed. Fr. Eric is one who says: "Writing and receiving Christmas card messages are an important part of my Christmas celebration." For young and old alike, the Christmas messages are a way of renewing connections with important people in their lives. The community itself receives Christmas cards in great numbers from family and friends. Many of them contain touching testimonials of love and support. These cards in recent years, are carefully mounted in a kind of scrapbook, which makes them easier to peruse and appreciate. All through the post-Christmas period, it is quite normal to see monks turning the pages of that special collection and making comments as they see the names of friends.

There is a kind of ebb and flow to the level of decoration and celebration, depending on the personnel on hand. When Br. Dominic was home, for instance, there was much more decoration around the grounds than there are now. Br. Lambert, for many years, has had a special crib and decorations in the library. Some monks are much more outgoing than others are. When they are at hand, more happens, even caroling in the town on occasion.

Christmas in the monastery is not the same as at home with Mother and Father and brothers and sisters around. The monks are not ashamed to say they miss their home, but they are quick to say that Christmas in the monastery is the next best thing.

A Musing on the Divine Office and Priorities

This was written for a Jewish friend.

I would like to share with you a resolution I made many years ago, and reflect on it a bit. In a recent exchange, we spoke of setting priorities in our daily scheduling. I have resolved that I will pray the morning prayers of Matins and Lauds sometime before I get up in the morning on those occasions when I cannot celebrate them with the community. That means that sometime during the night, depending on when I awake, I will pray the Office of Readings and Lauds. I try, by so doing, to make a statement to God and to myself that I value this time of prayer, and thereby avoid the risk of neglecting saying those prayers in a meaningful time of the day.

The daily official prayers that monks and priests obligate themselves to are known, generically, as the Divine Office, or sometimes as the Opus Dei (Work of God), or the Liturgy of the Hours. The prayers are a formalized collection of psalms, hymns and canticles interspersed with Scripture passages and prayers. The division of the prayers ranges through: Matins, Lauds, Prime, Terce, Sext, None, Vespers and Compline. A more current distribution is: Office of Readings, Morning Prayer, Noon Prayer, Vespers and Compline. In the monastery, these prayers are recited or sung together by members of the community in choir, and distributed throughout the day according to local custom.

Our custom at Saint Meinrad currently is: 5:30 a.m., Office of Readings and Morning Prayer (c. 40-50 minutes); 12:00 p.m., Noon Prayer; 5:00 p.m., Vespers; and Compline privately before bedtime. The Divine Office offers praise and thanksgiving to God throughout the day. This is done on our own behalf, but also on behalf of the whole Christian world and beyond. In a way, it is a prayer of humanity and, indeed, of all creation acknowledging God as Creator and provident sustainer of all creation.

In the *Rule of St. Benedict,* there is an expression: *Operi Dei nihil praeponatur* (Let nothing be preferred to the Work of God). So when one is at the Abbey, the priorities are already set. The hours of the Divine Office are set and there is seldom an excuse not to participate at the appointed time.

These times of prayer become a skeletal framework around which all other activities take place. When one is away from the monastery, though, it becomes much more difficult to establish a meaningful schedule. Individuals, depending on their own ingenuity, discipline, and/or zeal, will find time to pray the Hours.

I believe now there is much more sensitivity about trying to distribute the hours over the day. I remember a time when it was customary to say all the prayers in one sitting. It is of obligation, so not infrequently, men found themselves in the late hours of the evening scrambling to "get it in." I remember one parish priest who had a regular schedule of praying the whole thing every other night. About 11:15, he would pray today's prayers, then at midnight, he would pray those for the next day. This was regular routine for him. It fulfilled the law, but I was not edified.

I remember one time I chided a diocesan priest, who had somewhat reformed his religious practices, for saying Compline (night prayer) at 8 a.m. He brushed me off saying: "Look, kid, you should be damn good and glad that I am saying it at all." Actually, he had a heart of gold, but he accepted the obligation to pray the Divine Office as a burden. I believe that was the case of a lot of priests in the old days. I do not think that is the case today. Since the prayers are all in English, most priests enter into their prayer with more understanding and thoughtfulness.

I remember from my own personal experience, when I was visiting home as a young priest, that I had a hard time finding the time for Office. One evening I protested to my father that I had to get away to recite Matins, etc. It was close to 10 o'clock at night. He asked why I had not done that before. I said I had been too busy. He just shook his head in disbelief. He could not imagine himself saying morning prayers at 10 o'clock at night. It was after a few incidents like that that I determined that I would always pray my morning prayers in the morning. I have done that faithfully now for many years. On my recent sabbatical while I was away for six months, I never missed praying the morning prayer sometime in the middle of the night, 3, 4 or 5 a.m., whether I was at my brother's home, at a motel, or in the home of a friend. I also tried to pray the other hours throughout the day so that, even when I was away from the abbey, the Divine Office was a part of the structure of my day.

I believe this little essay started out as an example of how one sets priorities in one's life. I do not mean to brag. What I have done is no more than what I should be doing, but it does please me that I have found a living solution to a daily challenge to be faithful in my prayer, on my own behalf and of that of the whole world.

God's Will Be Done

A reflection given at the Shrine of Monte Cassino on October 2003.

St. Luke's description of the Annunciation is straightforward. The angel Gabriel proposes to Mary that she become the mother of the Messiah. Her simple protest that she was not married and also, perhaps, that she had vowed to remain a virgin, were quickly addressed by Gabriel's assuring her that that was no problem. "The Holy Spirit will come upon you, and the power of the Most High will overshadow you and you shall bear a son." With simple docility, she replied: "May it be it done unto me, according to your word." Mary stood ready to do God's will, whatever it may be.

That is the core of the message. Of course, there were a few other details that we would not want to gloss over, such as: "Hail, favored one! The Lord is with you." We interpret that as meaning. "Hail, full of grace," and ritualize it in the Hail Mary that we will recite so many times yet this afternoon. "Hail Mary, full of grace, the Lord is with you." The import of the greeting was not lost on Mary. She took some time to reflect on it—what it meant to be so greeted by a stranger. Once she was assured that he was a true messenger of God, she withdrew her hesitation. She was ready to do God's will, whatever it may be.

The world will never be the same again. If ever there was a pivotal moment in the history of mankind, this was it. Heaven and earth awaited her reply. Once given, she became the Mother of God and God had inserted Himself into our human condition, save sin. Who was this girl on whom so much depended? She was neither a mover nor shaker. She had never made a speech or given a sermon. Yet it was her "let it be done unto me," her readiness to do God's will, whatever it may be, that made her such a tower of strength in the history and mystery of our salvation.

I find this so fascinating. This simple young woman who never did anything more unusual than raise a child, with all the woes and joys that go with it, with a heart ready to do God's will whatever it may be, is the woman we speak in awe of as the Mother of God. Because of her special relationship with her son, and He with us, now we too call her Mother.

There may well be some among us facing important life decisions, even today. Let us keep them in mind as we pray the rosary, that, like Mary, they will be able to discern God's will for them and move on in peace.

She is particularly able to understand the ups and downs of our daily life. She, who on Calvary held Jesus' battered body in her bosom, will help us as church to bear the wounds of sin and discord that have plagued us and our church, especially in these latter days. As we greet Mary in our prayer of the rosary today, may we ask her to intercede for us, so that our wounds can be healed and that we learn the lesson she taught by her life of being ready to do God's will, whatever it may be.

A Monk Reflects on a Life of Prayer

I was requested to write this. It was used in a little publication for the annual financial report.

During a recent stay in the hospital, I was without my prayer books, but not without prayer. Short passages from the Psalms and the Gospels that I had memorized over the years kept me focused and comforted:

> *O God, come to my assistance.*
> *O Lord, make haste to help me.*

> *I will go to the altar of God, the God of my youth.*

> *O God, be gracious and bless us, and let your face shed its light upon us.*

It will soon be 60 years since I first began building my day around the regular round of prayer in church. While I was faithful to my duties, it was probably about 15 years before I truly embraced Divine Office as the core of my day. I came to make my own St. Benedict's expression that "nothing should be preferred to the Work of God."

> *My heart is ready, O God. My heart is ready.*

> *Hide not your face, O Lord. Hide not your face. It is your face I seek.*

St. Benedict, in his *Rule*, has some powerful insights on prayer, but no extended treatment. He urges that we be ever mindful of God's presence and listen to God calling us. Prayer follows. You breathe in awareness and breathe out praise and thanksgiving.

We participate in the daily Office no matter how we feel, striving to keep our minds in harmony with our voices. Over time, this practice begins to mold the character of the monk.

> *Show me, Lord, your way so that I may walk in your truth. Guide my heart to fear your name.*

Not my will but thine be done.

Anyone who spends much time here at Saint Meinrad soon learns the centrality of prayer. Whether in the monastery or the School, among the retreatants or visitors, prayer of one sort or another is part of the scene. Many of you who read this reflection can attest to this truth.

> *Send forth your light and your truth. Let these be my guide. Let them lead me to your holy mountain, the place where you dwell.*

I believe, Lord! Help my unbelief.

For me, it has been a joy to be part of the transition in our public prayer that allows students and visitors to participate freely. The shift from Latin to English has been a major factor. More dramatic has been the community's effort to enhance the prayer and prayer-space in our church so that participation is not the exception, but the expected.

> *Let the peoples praise you, O God. Let all the people praise you.*

I led a busy life working in the library for 51 years, but I am grateful beyond my fondest hopes that the daily round of prayer in church has formed the backbone of my day. Each day, with my body and my spirit, I try to deepen my awareness of my dependence on God, acknowledging it by prayers of thanksgiving, adoration, reparation and petition through the Psalms we sing and say.

> *Into your hands I commend my spirit.*

Truthfully, I do not look forward with enthusiasm to the diminishment of advanced age and infirmity that is seeping over my life. However, I have deep faith that I am on the right track with the prayer that has been instilled in me over the years. I pay homage to my Creator, the present and provident God, and I accept with thanksgiving the gift of life, even in its fading phases. I pray.

Ode to a Mosquito

This was written on the Island of Rhodes in September 1967.

There's a mosquito on my wall.
With a kind of brazen defiance
She rests there,
Pregnant, all unwittingly by me.

I resent this tiny creature,
Well within my reach.
Too heavy, alas, to fly higher.

She did pierce my virgin flesh
For her pleasure, wantonly.
What right had she to touch,
To caress,
then press
her vengeful lips to me?

Other lips
More tender,
More loving
I resisted manfully?

Where is the hurt she left?
Someplace surely she's left a sting
To trouble me.
Perhaps for days.

I spare this mite.
The hurt will pass.

The wound is in my flesh.
She has not touched my heart.

An Emergency Run

This was a communiqué to family and friends.

For over three weeks in the spring of 2003, I experienced a period of depressed heartbeats. My heartbeat ranged from the high 30s to the high 40s. The condition considerably impacted my energy. I felt washed out all the time and found it difficult to walk any distance without shortness of breath.

Throughout this whole period, I had ongoing attention with the staff of Health Service and Dr. Munning. A variety of tests were run and finally I was turned over to Dr. Dawkins, a heart specialist.

I was placed on a heart monitor. On the basis of the data that that instrument revealed, he scheduled me for a pacemaker on Monday, March 24, a simple, routine procedure. As it turned out, there was a major crisis and I went to that wall again. I can hardly believe that I was back home in my cell on Wednesday afternoon feeling, reasonably well and relaxed.

In the Jasper Memorial Hospital on Monday, I had been prepped for a 9 a.m. installation, and was waiting patiently to be taken to the operating room. About 9:15, a nurse came and took a sample of my blood. An hour later, the doctor came in to tell me that he had decided to wait a day because my blood was still too thin (due to blood-thinning medication I take to prevent blood clots). I was disappointed but knew I had no say, and it was in my best interest that the decision was made.

On leaving the hospital, I felt woozy but proceeded home. Once in my cell, I was so weak and uncomfortable that I took my own pulse. It was 26 beats per minute. I immediately called Fr. Anselm and all hell broke loose. After studying a report from the portable EKG machine, a decision was made that I needed to be gotten to the hospital. EMTs from our co-workers arrived; two nurses appeared; Fr. Prior anointed me at my request. By now, my heartbeats were at about 20.

The seriousness of the moment was not lost on me. In a brief lull, as we awaited the ambulance that had been summoned, I said that I would like to make a statement. In that awesome silence, I said: "If I die, please say he died a grateful man." I was so conscious at that hour of so many blessings in my life, not least of them being their careful attentions.

The ambulance arrived and suddenly there were three more people in my small cell. I was transported by ambulance to Jasper, sirens whining, and arrived in the emergency room, where a crew was prepared to meet me. Initial instructions were that I was to be taken to the operating room immediately. However, the doctor in ER said I was going nowhere. The situation had to be addressed immediately.

A temporary pacemaker was installed. Wires had to be inserted into my heart, but they did not attempt to make the cut that would have been needed to install a permanent one. They set the machine for an 80 heartbeat and my heart responded well.

The next day, Tuesday, I went back to surgery and the permanent pacemaker was installed, set for 60 beats per minute. The next day, Wednesday, I was sent home with a regular beat and feeling stronger. What an ordeal!

Thank you for your concern.

Daffodils in Spring

Bright faced daffodils bask in the morning sun.
Clumps of yellow blossoms wave shining faces
To all who pass by.

Comes now, out of season
A bitter frost that bows their heads.
Inch by inch they begin to sag
As the cold bites more deeply
Into their proud stems.

Alas, they lie there now
Bowed, broken
Still smiling
As life ebbs away.

How like the passing pleasures
That dot the landscape of our lives.
They smile a while
But cannot survive
The test of time
And the bite of bitter troubles
That, out of season,
Take hold of our troubled lives.

Justice Gone Awry

This is a fanciful response to a friend's not answering her phone. In this scenario, she is talking.

My friends frequently ask me where I go when I leave town rather regularly about twice a month. I am reluctant to tell them, but I need to record, if only for myself, what has come to pass. The fact is, I visit a friend in the state prison in Houston. As I say, we are friends, but I can't believe what has come to pass. Let me back up a little.

My father has made me chief executive of his affairs. He is quite elderly and, though of sound mind, does not feel up to the pressures of maintaining his portfolio and properties. It so happened that he wanted to sell off a rather sizeable piece of property in Florida and the burden of working out the details fell to me.

A man, whom I had never met, showed great interest in the property. After his initial contact, I said I would get back to him. I wanted to make sure I would get the best return for my father, and ultimately for my family. The gentleman became very insistent and called me frequently to advance his position. Actually, he became a nuisance to me. Over and over, I told him I would get in touch with him when I was ready to sell. It did not seem to register. Finally, I simply stopped answering the phone.

I had voice mail on my phone, but even though I seemed to be getting many calls, there was never a message. I complained to him once again and told him that if he continued to harass me I would go to the police. Well, after a two-week period when the phone rang dozens of times with no message, I figured I would fix him and reported the problem to the police.

I know what prompted me to do this, but I will always regret the decision. They began an investigation. After months and what seemed forever, they discovered that the calls were originating in Indiana and not Texas. It seemed that the calls were coming from two numbers. Further investigation showed that they were from a priest friend who was a member of a monastic community there. The numbers, it turned out, were for the phones in his office and cell.

As soon as I was made aware of that, I told them I did not want to press charges and they should just forget about it. I had no quarrel with my friend and certainly did not want press the issue any further, but the police were not willing to go along with that. They said that it was no longer my right to determine the outcome. This was a case of harassment across state lines and, therefore, was a serious federal offense.

Can you imagine my distress at this outcome? My friend claimed he was only trying to get in touch. He freely admitted that he might have overdone it. According to him, he began to worry if something untoward had happened to me. He knew I seldom left Austin for more than a week at a time. He said he was haunted by the feeling that he might have been dialing the wrong number, because he could not recognize my voice on the recorder. He said it was very gruff and unwelcoming, which he felt was not characteristic. Since I live alone, he worried that I might have become ill and need help. In any case, he called every evening for almost two weeks and sometimes several times in the evening.

Now it was out of my hands. It was explained to me that the law was very strict to protect the innocent and to discourage using the phone to hassle anyone. It never came to trial in court. The embarrassment and bad publicity for me, for him, and for his community led him to accept judgment with a minimum sentence.

He has ended up in Houston. The prison administrators are very reasonable in allowing him special privileges. They recognize that justice may have gone awry here. Legally, they had to keep him incarcerated, but they had the leeway of allowing him to have Mass once a week and function somewhat unofficially as a chaplain.

He has quite a following and has interested a number of the inmates to study the *Rule of St. Benedict* with him.

Well, there it is. I can't believe the mess I have caused, but I live with it. I try to visit him twice a month and drop him a note every week. He does not seem to have any rancor over the situation, though he is not afraid to say how upset he has been over what has come to pass.

Given his age, it is likely he will die in prison.

In Time of Distress

I was asked to provide a text for a possible musical arrangement. It was put to music with a four-part harmony. The text is unashamedly drawn from the psalms.

Comfort your people, Lord,
Comfort them.
Their hearts are heavy
Their cares many,
As they bear the burden of the day.
Comfort your people, Lord,
Comfort them.

Heal the sick,
Ease the pain of those preparing to die.
Comfort the sorrowing.
Show them your way.

Soften the hearts of those
Who make strife all the day long.
So that they may enjoy your peace,
And give you glory all the day.

Comfort your people, Lord,
Comfort them.

Ready their hearts,
Prepare them to do your will,
So that they may walk in your truth.
Guide their hearts to fear your name.

Liken them to the tree
Planted by flowing waters,
So that all they do shall prosper,
As they ponder your law day and night.

Comfort your people, Lord,
Comfort them.

Lift up their hearts,
Lift them out of the darkness
Of selfishness and sin
Into your own saving light.

Lead them to your holy mountain,
To the place where you dwell,
So that they may be free from sin,
And praise your name all the day.

Comfort your people, Lord,
Comfort them.
Their hearts are heavy,
Their cares many,
As they bear the burden of the day.
Comfort your people, Lord,
Comfort them.

One Last Kiss

This piece was written one night when I felt I was dying. I scribbled it on an envelope, barely legible the next day. It filled a need to say goodbye to friends. The title was from an old song in the '50s. The words were rattling around in my head. I learned only later that the original song was marking the end of an illicit relationship.

The time has come.
I feel it in my bones.
Many signs whisper:
"it is time to let go; to leave undone things begun."

The time has come to quit this place,
The space where I have lived and loved.

I beg the grace
Of your embrace
Before I go.

One more kiss
To say:
"I love you so,"
Before I go away.

I want you to remember
That I have loved you dearly,
And I care.

Please, now,
One last kiss
Before we say:
"Goodbye."

The Cost of Listening to My Stories

My stories were first shared on micro-cassette tapes. This was an imagined scenario. Mike had the cassettes and had been eager to listen to them. This essay was an imagined excuse for his not getting back in touch with me promptly. The fact is, I was eager to have his approval.

I can see it now. There you are, all bandaged up in a hospital bed at St. Vincent's. Your right leg is in a cast and dangling from a pulley attached to the ceiling. At least you are alive, but not much more. You can remember being med-evaced from Bedford hospital to St. Vincent's in Indianapolis, but have only vague notions of the ambulance ride, with sirens whining, from I-65 to the Bedford facility. They moved you on, assuring you your needs could be better met in Indianapolis.

You had listened to the first tape in Evansville. Just north of New Albany at a rest stop, you changed from tape two to three. You were right in the middle of the story on various scenarios when the tape ran out. Eager to hear more, but not willing to stop and make the change properly, you proceeded to try to change to cassette four while driving. The car was in cruise control, the highway was flat and straight and no vehicles in sight. It was a mistake. Fiddling with both hands on that little recorder, you got only halfway through the process when you lost control of the car.

After police and EMTs extracted you from the jumbled mess that had been your car and while waiting for the ambulance to transport you, you could hear the police puzzling over how you had gotten so entwined in audio tape. You were not forthcoming. I know you did not lie to them, but you were not entirely upfront about the tape. That sordid little detail the insurance company would suck up, since they might have to replace the tangle of metal stuck in the ditch, which had been your Lexus.

The nurses said that, in your less-lucid moments, you kept asking how the scenarios turned out. They didn't know what to say. Fortunately, I have a copy I can share when you are further along in your recovery.

How I Saved a Little and Lost a Bundle

I grew up during the Depression. That has colored a number of attitudes that I have and things that I do. I am not obsessed over it, but I do shut off lights all over the place, day and night. "Maybe," I say to myself. "Maybe it will extend the length of life of the bulb or save a few cents for the electricity. I suggest this attitude greatly influenced my not turning on lights and suffering the consequences.

It was June 3, 2002, around 9 o'clock in the evening. I was on my way to my office when I remembered the e-mail that announced that shrimp was available in the pantry on a first come, first serve basis. I headed for the pantry, but did not turn on the lights to walk down the office corridor. I knew my way. Had done something similar countless times before. I felt a twinge of guilt that I should be helping myself before the real staff had a chance to sample the goodies. I had pretty much resolved that, if there were only a few, I would pass them up.

What I found was a huge, ice-laden bowl of luscious-looking jumbo shrimp. I helped myself to five of them on a little paper plate with a generous glob of the special sauce that so enhances the taste of shrimp. I planned to go from there to my office, where I could enjoy the minor feast at leisure. I never made it.

I had taken only a few steps into the dimly lit office area when I hit an obstacle. Actually, it was a chair. I walked into it and literally went flying over it. The next thing I knew I was stunned on the floor, still holding an empty paper plate in my right hand. I could not move my left arm. I knew immediately that I had done something foolish and that I was not out, but injured.

Whoozy, I managed to get to a desk and chair from which I could call for help. Fr. Anselm, a trained nurse, was summoned. In the meantime, I found the lights and crawled around on the floor with my left arm dangling, retrieving the scattered shrimp. I ate them without benefit of sauce or much joy, but at least I did not let them get away. This was the beginning of an ordeal.

I had crushed the bone-ball at the upper end of the humerus that fits into the socket of my shoulder. I was not put in a cast nor did they do any surgical procedure on me. My arm was put in a sling and I waited for the healing to take place.

There is a lot packed into that "waited." There was much internal bleeding and my arm went from blue to black and stayed that way for several weeks. I could not take care of myself, but I also did not want to burden the brethren. I didn't change my clothes for a week at a time when one of the infirmarians would give me a shower and dress me. I did not lie in my bed for a month. I sat in my chair through the night.

I began physical therapy within a few days of the accident and kept it up for over six months. I now have about 90% use of that arm. I will go to my grave with reminders of that evening when I lusted after a few shrimp and changed my life forever.

I may have saved a few pennies. Who can figure the costs to me personally and to the monastery? There were hospital bills, doctor bills, prescription pills, six months with a physical therapist, and lost time. All for opting not to turn on the lights.

Response at Retirement Dinner

Talk given on May 18, 2001.

Thank you most sincerely for those words and for this occasion. I have tried to be an engaged colleague in this noble educational endeavor. I have cared deeply about the role of the library and its services. I have no doubt that the whole enterprise helped to shape who I am today.

It would, perhaps, be most gracious of me to sit at this point. May I beg your indulgence for a few musings? I apologize for reading my remarks. They could be more heartfelt expressed *ex tempore*, but there might be greater risk of undo expansion of these words.

Years ago, it was the custom in the Saint Meinrad monastic community to offer golden jubilarians the opportunity to say a few words. It is no longer an option for reasons my own remarks here may provide a clue, On one occasion, Fr. Eberhard noted that he had been so impressed by the remarks of the first jubilarian he had heard that he thought he should record the essence of the remarks for when he would have to do something similar 50 years down the road. The next year he had a similar experience, and the next. After 25 years, he had a list of 25 items, way too many, so he began to cut them down one at a time for the next 25 years. Now when it was his opportunity to speak, he had none left. Everyone breathed a sigh of relief, aware of his tendencies, until he added that, in which case, he would speak for a few moments on the meaning of jubilee in the Old Testament. He proceeded to do so for over a half hour. Trust me. I will not pull a Fr. Eberhard on you, but, then, there is a certain risk taken, when you allow an old man to speak.

First, I want to express my appreciation to the administrations down the years that allowed me to advance my professional status as a librarian. I was able to participate in state and national associations, and to keep up in my field by attending workshops and programs of continuing education. My active involvement with the American Theological Library Association was personally transforming.

In 1947, as a young monk preparing my chart for solemn profession, I inscribed in the initial "I," which I illuminated, poorly I must add, the words of

Jesus from the Last Supper, *Ut omnes unum sint* (That they all may be one). Under the influence of my recent readings, I dedicated my monastic life to Christian unity, at a time when I could not name ten non-Catholic persons of my acquaintance, nor, given the nature of the life I was entering at that time, was there much likelihood that I would ever have occasion to know more. One of the great consolations of my life is that I spent the crowning years of my professional career, for close to 20 years, working almost daily in an ecumenical environment, with non-Catholic theological librarians, not engaging in theological discussion, but in trying to advance the Kingdom by improvement in library service. Few here had any clue of the extent of my involvement, and endearment, with librarians of other religious persuasions, in all the major divinity schools throughout the country. For me, that whole experience was a miracle of grace for which I will be forever thankful. I share it here with you now to explain a glow in my heart that goes beyond telling and that contributes even now to the joy of my life.

I should like to mention two moments, almost evenly spaced over my career, that involve two persons not of our communities that greatly touched me and had a great influence on the direction our library has taken. I choose these stories from among so many because they are less known and yet important to the history of the library, and to my story.

First is Miss Katherine Skinner. At the time that I was appointed to the library in 1949, we were in dire need of direction in the organizing of our uncataloged collection of over 60,000 volumes, if we were ever to seek accreditation. Miss Skinner left her position as a senior cataloger at Yale to come and supervise the major task of putting our house in order. She started May 1, 1950. By the way, I did not hire her; she was hired before I became the library director. She came with elaborate plans for setting up teams of catalogers, whom she hoped to train and supervise. She was immediately deflated when she was given a desk and pencils and asked to set to work.

Undaunted, she began. She did train a few of us to her very high standards that, in time, made our catalog a model of academic excellence comparable to any. She was very professional. Very demanding. The rule of thumb without exception was that every card to go into any catalog had to be proofread, and no known error be allowed to stand without correction. This was a standard we kept religiously, though errors did creep in, until the catalog was closed in 1990. Miss Skinner stayed with us four years. They were reasonably happy years, but she experienced a good bit of frustration at the lack of vision, on the part of the movers and shakers. Around that time, I requested doubling the $1,000 budget for books and periodicals, only to be told that the monks hadn't read all the books that we had yet, and what we had would do. Miss Skinner's parting shot, in the very last lines of her final report, went something like this: this library will never become what it should be in this institution until it begins to be appreciated and supported as a place as important to the life here on the Hill as the kitchen and the powerhouse. I would like to say things changed. They didn't, at least very much, until accreditation became more of a motivator.

The second person is Dr. David Kaser. I credit him with helping to move along the decision to build a new library. From about 1966 on, I had urged the need for more space for our library program. My appeals went unheeded. I had spoken at length with every architect interviewed spelling out our needs. Finally, Victor Christ-Janer was hired. He promulgated a list of space priorities for the Hill. The library was ranked 15th on the list. I was devastated. Six or seven years later, things hadn't changed much, though I continued the drumbeat. Enter Dr. David Kaser. He was a distinguished, internationally respected library-building consultant. I had made his acquaintance, and had an opportunity to hire him to lead up a team to assess the state of our library program. The report, affectionately known as the Kaser Report, was funded by a Lilly grant. This automatically put the report in the public forum and gave it clout. Dr. Kaser took responsibility for the area covering the library physical facilities. After some passing swipes, he concluded: "On a scale of A to F, Saint Meinrad's library facilities score an ignominious F." Almost overnight, the library jumped from 15th to second on the priorities list.

Shortly after that, during a meeting with the architects, I made bold to suggest that a philosophical distinction be made. In the order of eminence, monastery first; library second; in the order of time, equal, i.e. to be built simultaneously. I won't say what I was told to do with my mouth. I am happy to say that later, at the suggestion of a young faculty member, that it would make sense to do the two buildings at the same time; the monastic chapter voted to do so. It was done, and we enjoy the buildings we have today. Dr. Kaser's incisive report greatly facilitated the decision to move forward, and his later assistance in preparing the program document to guide the architects contributed much to the quality of the building we now enjoy.

I will conclude these ramblings with a word about staffing the library. In the early days, the librarian had absolutely no say about staff. Persons were appointed and removed without consultation. At one point, ten or 12 years after I took over the library, I counted over 50 monks who had come and gone as library help. Even Br. Lambert, coming in 1958, was already the fourth person assigned as my assistant. Happily, he remained and came to be a partner in every project and activity of the library ever since. Fr. Placidus, whom I succeeded, worked in the library for about 15 years before he retired. Fr. Philip Mahin received library training, and even taught library science at Indiana State University. He was an excellent cataloger and colleague until his premature death in 1971.

Ruth Ann Denning was the first person I actually hired, shortly after Fr. Philip died. There is practically no activity of the library that she has not had a hand in. She was of great assistance to me when I served as president of ATLA and while I was, at the same time, heavily involved in the practical details of planning the new library. Fr. Justin had a few years at it. Br. Placid, now of blessed memory, 14 years. Mary Ellen Seifrig was orginally hired by me to help in my work for ATLA. It was a part-time position that she filled with great efficiency and care. Later, she brought a willing spirit and intelligent competence to a full-time position over ten years ago. Br. Lambert, Ruth Ann and Mary Ellen are here tonight, and it would be unthinkable for me to accept your recognition without acknowledging their hard work, their unfailing dedication to this institution, and their unflagging support to me. They were the cause of much joy in my life. Please recognize them.

This may be my last hurrah, but the library goes on. I urge your continued support of the library program. Give Ms. Zakharov and her staff the support and backing they need as they continue to face the challenges of our changing world.

Thank you.

Some Reflections on a Special Journey

This was written in August 2001 after a July trip to Guatemala. It was shared with a few friends who had been on pilgrimage to Israel with me in 1999.

For the past couple of years, I have had an exceptional opportunity to make a kind of pilgrimage to friends, important in my life. With each of them, I had the chance to speak a bit about the meaning of life, the importance of values, my gratitude for the love of friendship, and to say good-bye.

One such friend, Fr. Thomas McSherry, made it possible for me to visit him at his mission in Santiago, Guatemala. On the way there and back, I had the opportunity to greet and be with several people whom I had met in Israel. Lorena Valesquez-Ampie, her daughter, Ana, and a friend, Hilda. They welcomed me in Guatemala City with open arms. Overall, I spent three nights with them. They picked me up at the airport, drove me to and from Santiago, drove me to Antigua, fed me, and got me on the plane to return to the States. They could not have been warmer or kinder. It was a real thrill to be able to see them again, a prospect that had never entered my head until this venture made it possible to plan. My encounters with them provided me with an exquisite joy that will nourish me as I continue my journey.

I went to Santiago, Guatemala, one of a number of towns and villages perched on the mountains around Lake Atitlan. For the most part Santiago is a Tzutuhil community of Mayan Indians. Fr. McSherry has been their pastor for 17 years. He is an alumnus of our School of Theology ('71), where we became friends. He was planning to come back to the States July 31. He said he would like me to see what he had been able to do. Actually, he paid my way. He probably has about 10,000 parishioners in six districts of Santiago and another church he serves in Cerro de Oro, about ten miles away.

I was in awe from the first moment I got there. The beauty of the landscape is truly breathtaking. The combination of Lake Atitlan, the mountains and the three volcanoes is very impressive. In Santiago, the view of the San Pedro volcano is immediately in front of the veranda of the parish complex. In Cerro de Oro, the view of the lake and the surrounding mountains from the porch of his rectory was awesome.

The simplicity and the warmth of hospitality of the Mayans were immediately remarkable. The reverence and respect they have for Fr. McSherry is obvious and impressive. Many of the homes of the natives are hovels or shacks, but their colorful clothing seems fresh and clean. In physical stature, few are more than five feet tall. Most of the women continue to wear long skirts and colorful blouses and carry almost universally a *paraje* or *reboso*, an extra shawl or scarf-like vestment. They wear it and use it in a variety of ways that are quite creative. The women, especially, are adept in carrying containers of one sort or another on their heads. For larger loads, there seems to be a base on which the baskets sit. Some women wear a colorful headdress. Most of the laundering is done in the lake or in streams, to which they walk with the laundry balanced on their heads.

While the women have maintained their traditional dress, only some men have. The men and boys, for the most part, dress as we do. I noticed quite a number of girls in uniforms, much as you would see in the States with blouse, short skirt and knee socks. This was in such high contrast to all the other women, I wondered if someone was trying to break down the native dress.

The main highways are quite modern and in good repair. Once one leaves the highway, the roads are not paved and leave much to be desired. In the cities, the streets are very narrow and passage is hazardous. There are no sidewalks, so people traffic and auto and truck traffic vie for space, each at their own risk.

One sees people walking the highways in considerable numbers. Walking is the main mode of transportation. There are buses that ply the highways. Some enter the villages. A very common way of getting around is a taxi of sorts. Pickup trucks are provided with a reinforced bar over the truck-bed. People stand in the truck-bed and hold on to the central bar as best they can. It is not unusual to see trucks with 15 to 20 people riding in this way bouncing down treacherous backroads or highways. Most Indians do not own automobiles, though there are some. If a family owns a vehicle at all, it is likely to be a truck.

Many of the Tzutuhil are bilingual, speaking their native language and Spanish. The language of the liturgy is a mixture of both. A large pool of musicians who play guitars and other instruments are available from which to draw for the music at Mass. At the Masses I attended, there were around ten players, plus a choir of around 30 ladies.

At a Thursday afternoon Mass, the church was packed. Collections were taken up, and on that day, which is a regular ritual on Thursdays, around 50 women filed up to the altar to offer a packet of corn that would later be distributed to widows of the parish. At Santiago, a catafault is present at every Mass and is incensed and sprinkled. In the recessional procession, a line of at least 30 men filed out with small white sacks in which they carried the Eucharist for communion to the sick. The congregation seems quite devotional and reverent. Children and dogs ply the aisles without much ado.

I accompanied Father to an anointing of a dying man, who later died. The funeral rites were held on Sunday, after which there was a funeral procession to the cemetery, about three quarters of a mile away.

The homily is delivered in Spanish, followed by a translation by a native in their dialect. The liturgies are very formal, with a master of ceremonies who directs the various movements throughout the church. There is an entrance procession that includes the lectors, the cantors, and the Eucharistic ministers, who numbered about 20 on the days that I attended. Weekday Masses have all these ceremonies, including incense at the entrance, at the Gospel, at the offertory (including the altar, the cross, the priest and the congregation), during the consecration, and at the end of Mass for the ritual around the catafault and recessional. The Thursday I attended, the Mass lasted an hour and 25 minutes. People remain in church after mass for parish announcements and personal devotions. The announcements, in lieu of a parish bulletin, are made by one of the administrators of the parish.

The parish activities are thoroughly organized and managed. About 15 heads of services gather for staff meetings twice a day, at 8 o'clock and at 1 p.m. to keep everyone updated and on the same page. The walls of the meeting room are lined with work sheets on which the schedule of activities were clearly marked out for a week ahead. Issues arising between meetings are dealt with. Agenda items are submitted on color-coded paper, green for guests, blue for the church in Cerra de Oro, and black for Santiago. There are as many as 60 people involved in the administration of the parish.

Widows are particularly vulnerable financially. The parish provides corn to them, as mentioned above, and provides them with space for business for tourists, i.e. handicraft for sale. Because of assassinations of a number of the men over time, the widows are a serious concern of the parish. I was privileged to attend a luncheon where five of them represented their group. It was meant to involve them in an opportunity to say their thanks to Fr. McSherry. The ladies were practically speechless throughout the meal, but when given the opportunity to say goodbye and thank Father, some went on for as much as five minutes. One of the ladies had had two husbands assassinated. I could not understand them, but their words were translated to Spanish for Father and to English for me. I was so touched I could not keep back my tears. I was a basket case after they left. They have no assurance that the next pastor will continue their program. They were most grateful for what had been done for them and were reasonably anxious about the future of their project. Their expressions were earnest and were delivered with an animation not evident throughout the meal.

The Mass on Sunday, July 23, my last day there, was a phenomenon of the religious culture. The bishop of the diocese was there for confirmation of around 230 young people. I have never seen a more packed church. The pews were filled, but so were the aisles, where men, women and children sat shoulder to shoulder. In fact, there was no aisle left. A rough estimate put the numbers close to 3,000. The parents, sponsors and confirmees alone would take the number over 1,000. The Mass took two and a half hours.

Since Father would be leaving soon, a number of meals were planned to treat the guests, and then to allow them an opportunity to express their thanks. I had the opportunity to be present for several such testimonials of appreciation. The dioceses of Oklahoma practically underwrites the program, so he had funds to do wonderful things for the parish and for many needy and hurting people. In Santiago, he repaired the church and the rectory. In Cerro de Oro, he built a beautiful church and a huge rectory that also serves as the parish office complex. He was able to build homes for a number of his parishioners, and made it possible for serious medical problems to be addressed for individuals in Guatemala City. I was on the brink of tears most of the time, as I realized that he is letting go of so much that he has poured his heart into, over the years. It is truly inspiring to see what a person can do with zeal and financial support.

Fr. McSherry has, in a counter-cultural way, integrated women into everything. They read, they play in music groups, they cantor, they translate from Spanish to Tzutuhil (one of 24 Mayan dialects). They function as Eucharist ministers. The parish administrator is a woman. It is not sure that his successor, not yet appointed, will allow that to continue. The uncertainty about the future only added to the pain for both Father and the administrators of the parish.

For all that the visit did for me, I am most grateful. I am also very happy that I was able to be there for him in these painful days. We had some very good discussions and I have no doubt I was a boon to him in this time of need. I cried more than he did, though, and one time after a few testimonials by representatives of a group of widows whom he helped, as mentioned above, I was no good to him at all. After they left, I grabbed on to him while my body shook with emotion. I had been so touched by their gratitude and their pain.

I could go on. I was there from Tuesday, July 17, to Sunday July 22, 2001. I hope what I have reported imparts some little information. Even more, I hope these few words convey some of the roller coaster ride my heart went on. The love of friendship was deeply confirmed. I experienced awe at rare beauty and abject poverty. I was touched by the gratitude shown by a people who had been well served. I suffered the feeling of pain from separation and the sense of loss with Father's parting. I will go to my grave a richer man for having had these joyful, sad and touching moments. Bless God.

Br. Clement Seichter, O.S.B.

Br. Clement was a very senior brother when I came to the monastery. He was no longer able to work, but he spent many hours in prayer in church. I was always very edified to see him sitting in his regular place in front of the statue of St. Joseph. I do not recall ever seeing him with a prayer book.

In his latter days, shortly before he was confined to bed, he began to be a little addled. On one occasion, a sign went up saying that we wanted to keep watch with him 24 hours a day. It seems he asked someone for a match. He said he had cleaned up his garden and wanted to burn the trash. The trash it turned out was all the furniture of his cell. A match there might easily wipe out the monastery. I got to know Br. Clement during the many hours of watching that I put in over a period of six months or so. He had no idea why he had so much company.

Once he was no longer considered a threat and the watching stopped, I continued to visit him. Although he was not all there, he had some lovely pious expressions that impressed me. After he had died, I wrote some of them down on 3 x 5 cards. Because at one point Brother had noted that he and Fr. Abbot Ignatius were very special friends and that Fr. Abbot would come to him for a blessing before he went on his longer trips, I thought it would be nice to show my notes to Fr. Abbot and did.

He called me to his office after he had read them to thank me and to talk a bit about Br. Clement. Among other things, he remarked that on his *Bona Opera*, an instrument of good resolutions for Lenten practice submitted by the monks to the abbot every Ash Wednesday, Br. Clement put down that he would visit the cemetery twice a day during Lent. At the time, he took such short steps that the walk to the cemetery must have taken close to a half hour.

I was so edified by that that I began putting in my *Bona Opera* each year that I would visit the cemetery to pray for the dead once each day. That was in 1945. I am sure that I never mentioned this practice to anyone for almost 50 years. It was a private and personal devotion prompted by the piety of that old, addled monk.

Then, for the next few years, before I had to give up the practice because of physical disability, I would collar anyone within reach to tell him or her the story of how a young, idealistic monk was so touched by the old man's piety that he imitated him in a small way for almost the rest of his life. The power of good example continues to touch hearts. That confused old man so touched me that I continue to admire him and try to imitate his devotion to this day.

Homily in the Archabbey Church: Transfiguration

This homily was given on February 28, 1999.

We are all aware of the place accreditation plays in our lives. We want to see a license, a badge, a uniform, or a diploma from an accredited school. These formalities authenticate the right of a person or institution to act officially in our society. Just this week, I heard an advertisement for a bartending school. We were assured it was fully accredited. Many of us in this community know full well the struggle we had to get our high school, our college, and, finally, our school of theology accredited—it took over 30 years.

The Transfiguration was a kind of accreditation for Jesus. It provided official recognition from God that Jesus was acting authentically. The apostles needed that assurance. Jesus had just told them that he was to die a most shameful death. In a culture where honor was treasured, power venerated, and shame most to be avoided, this recognition of Jesus by God was most important. Not just for the apostles. The early faith community for which Matthew was writing needed such assurances, even as we do ourselves. That Jesus had special powers no one denied. In that Mediterranean culture, such powers gave him high standing despite his low origins—a carpenter's son from Nazareth. Where did he get His power? Some, you recall, suggested from the Devil and were going about saying so.

The Transfiguration speaks of a spiritual world, and the voice from heaven clarifies things further by declaring: "This is my beloved son; hear Him." A consoling message for those who might feel ashamed to a follow a crucified leader and who were (and are) being asked to put their lives in His hands.

In the first Gospel, Matthew is at pains to depict Jesus as the new Moses. He does that subtly throughout, but in this Transfiguration scene, he shows that Jesus is in conversation with Moses, the great teacher and leader of God's people, and Elijah, the prophet. This nuance was not lost on the apostles.

It has been said that the Church inserts this Gospel passage here early in Lent to bolster our faith in Him for whom and with whom we are proceeding along this journey toward Easter. Lent or not, though, this transfiguration story is worthy of our meditation and contemplation. Mystics of our tradition have made much of the words "only Jesus." In context, of course. they tell us that the vision is over and, once again, they are alone with Jesus. In the culture of *lectio, meditatio, oratio,* and *contemplatio,* being alone with Jesus takes on a very personal meaning and a call to focus our lives only on Jesus, and Him crucified.

Mull over this Gospel passage. It has much to teach us. It ought to encourage us to follow more faithfully the One from God, the New Moses, who invites us to take up our cross and follow Him. Moses trusted in God despite all the trials. Jesus trusted in God despite the great trials that He was put through. The early apostolic community was urged not to be put off by the shame of the cross. God's fidelity to Jesus more than made up for the pain He had endured. We, too, must trust in God despite the bad things that come our way and fill our day. Would a voice from heaven say of you or me: this is my beloved son or daughter?

Some of that we do here and now as we offer this Sacrifice of Praise to the Father in His memory. We re-offer ourselves to be His followers at this altar, and approach that altar to be nourished for the journey by His Body and Blood. We do not have to be mystics to be in great awe at what we are about. If we do it right, it might just change our lives.

Br. Placid McIver, O.S.B.

A memorial in connection with the funeral of Br. Placid McIver, O.S.B., November 12, 1925-April 29, 2001

On behalf of the whole community, I offer sincere condolences to the niece and nephews of Br. Placid, and to his many friends.

In recent years, some such memorial as this has been added to the prayers for our deceased confreres. It provides an opportunity to give a personal flavor to the burial rites. I feel honored to be able to offer a few thoughts about Br. Placid, aware that others in the community were closer to him and knew him better.

Because we sometimes wait until a monk has died before we say the nice things about him that we do, I offered a slightly different version of these remarks to Br. Placid over a year ago. My hope was that he might be assured that his wholesome goodness was recognized and appreciated. He thanked me and smiled.

St. Gregory the Great, in his second Dialogue introduced St. Benedict to the world with the classic expression, a play on the word *benedictus*: *There was a man of venerable life, blessed by grace and blessed in name. He was called Benedict.* The venerable disciple of St. Benedict, whom we mourn, was Placid by grace and Placid in name. No one adjective or even group of adjectives would be adequate to characterize Br. Placid, but placid is certainly most apt. He was a peaceful, calm and calming man.

Of his family most of us knew little, except for his mother who had moved to Evansville, and who enjoyed Br. Placid's attentions in her declining years. She was feisty. Not always patient with ineptitude. Brother was called on a number of times to go to Evansville to calm the waters. His devotion to his mother was apparent. He made many sacrifices to visit her as often as he could. They were an interesting pair. Not a lot of open affection was shown, but there was an obvious love and devotion to each other. They both were serious readers, and one can only imagine their heady conversations as they discussed their latest readings. When she died, a long shadow was cast across Brother's life.

There were other such shadows, as men in the community that Brother was devoted to passed on. One of the mysteries of Br. Placid, who was not demonstratively affectionate, was his ability to have loyal friendships with the most diverse people. They recognized his unselfish goodness and welcomed his caring kindness. For years, Br. Placid planned detailed educational vacations from one end of the country to the other with various members of the community. He probably visited every president's tomb open to the public. I have little doubt that Brother could recite the names of all the presidents, indicate where they were buried and why. He could add some interesting nosegay about each one's life and work. He particularly enjoyed trips with Br. Rene, who was also quite a history buff. Br. Placid missed him after Br. Rene's final illness and death, though trips with Br. Andrew helped to carry on the tradition in these recent years. It is worthy of note that he died on just such a journey, not on the way out but on the way home.

For many years, Brother took long walks with Brother Casmir. It was quite touching to see them continue to "walk" after Br. Casmir was confined to his motorized cart. When later, Brother Casmir was somewhat confined to his infirmary cell, Br. Placid visited him every day. Losing such good friends cast long shadows across his life.

Brother did not wear his emotions or his religious devotion on his sleeve. Yet he had deep feelings and tender devotion. There was nothing superficial about his religious commitment. He took his monastic life seriously and lived the life. Br. Placid loved God, but he showed it mostly by his actions.

Not everyone in the community was aware of the countless little services Br. Placid rendered day by day. He typed for those who couldn't. He delivered books personally to those who found it hard to get to the library. He was an easy mark for those who needed substitutes to read at Office, wait or read at table. He was always ready and willing and dependable.

Before Brother came to the monastery, he had a job as a secretary to some mogul of the Santa Fe Railroad in downtown Chicago. There he became accustomed to picking up and delivering mail several times a day. At the library, he seemed obsessed by mail. Four or five times a day, he would make his way to the mailroom from the library. The staff kidded him that he had the mail box wired, so quick was he to pick up and deliver any piece that got in the outbox. He literally paced the floor awaiting the truck with the morning delivery. No piece was left undated, no box left unopened. The ladies in the mailroom knew him first-hand.

The library, of course, was not his only job in the course of his monastic life. He had served many years as the secretary to the abbot. He had two stints in the Development Office. He was for many years a clerk in the Scholar Shop. Throughout all those years, he reached out to people in his caring way, gathering another public in as friends.

Although his head was filled with unbelievable minutiae, he was eager to philosophize about events. In his wisdom, he tried to perceive how things fit into God's plan. When speaking of God's providence, which he often did, his face would wince up in that way that we do when talking through tears. He constantly looked for supernatural meaning in human and cosmic event.

It was such a pleasure to listen to him. He was a voracious and fast reader, and seemed to be able to store and categorize whatever he read. He was equally at home discussing the Civil War, the American presidents, the politics of the hour, the Ming Dynasty in China, the Mayans of Guatemala, the geo-political status of the Holy Land throughout history, sequoias of California, the archeology of the

Grand Canyon and on and on. What more can one say? There were few topics that one could bring up that he could not discuss intelligently, and indeed add significant information and comment.

I regret to say, though, that I know not a single essay that Br. Placid has written about any of the topics that he could expound so eloquently. We all remember the several memorials of his friends, which he wrote and delivered here so movingly.

What a pleasure it has been to live and work with Br. Placid in brotherhood these many years. I believe his presence, his friendship and his grace enriched the whole Saint Meinrad community. He was gracious, kind, loyal, thoughtful and upbeat. On each of these words, there could be a story. He was supportive and caring. It would have been difficult not to like him. He was indeed a placid man, a Christ figure in our midst. A long shadow has come into our lives for his passing.

May he rest in peace.

Homily for the Funeral for Br. Vincent Brunette, O.S.B.

The gospel readnig was from John 11:17-36

Our sincere condolences to the family and friends of Br. Vincent. Your presence here is testimony to the quality of his life. Please know that we, his brothers in the community, share your sorrow, and in faith your joy that Br. Vincent has gone to a better place.

Br. Vincent never created a family, but he was a family man. He never raised children, but he had the virtues of patience, compassion and steadfast love of a parent. He seldom ever had occasion to speak publicly, but his life and example spoke eloquently of how one loves God and neighbor. We have gathered, some with great pain, to bury his body. His spirit remains with us and his soul has been taken up to that place where Jesus is, and where He rewards with eternal life those who take up their cross and follow Him. Indeed, Br. Vincent never created a family, but he was a family man and we are all part of that family.

Although requiring care in these latter days, he was a caregiver in many ways, including caring for his parents in their waning hours, an ordeal that went on for several years. That is when the family got to see his mettle. From Mondays to Fridays each week, he did all the humble chores and met their every need, as best he could, including meals and laundry. That he loved his parents was shown by his patience. Though some may have thought it a lark for him to be home all week, in truth, it was one of the more difficult periods of his generous life. On the other hand, the caring infirmary staff, and they are most caring, will attest to the unobtrusive patience he manifested in bearing the burdens of his own waning years. It was a joy to care for him.

A touching story in the life of Jesus was His affection for Mary, Martha and Lazarus. Although much is left to our imagination, we easily gather that they were very special people in His life. That He had a genuine love for them is patent. It is providential that the Scriptures have preserved for us some special moments in their lives, including coping with death.

No question, Mary and Martha loved each other, but there was a kind of sibling rivalry between them for the affection of Jesus.

Even before their beloved brother had died, and was buried, they had sent for Jesus. They went into mourning. Word got to Martha that Jesus was on the way. She ran out to meet him along the road. They had a brief encounter. Jesus evokes from her an expression of faith in his power to bring Lazarus back to life. Not just to eternal life, but to restore his natural life. Martha, for her part, sensitive to Mary's love, unselfishly slipped back to the house to tell her that Jesus was near. What a wonderful example of unselfish love. Her love for both Jesus and Mary impelled her to hasten their encounter. If there was rivalry there, Martha was able to rise above it.

The encounter between Jesus and Mary follows. It was very emotional. They both wept; she at his feet. The Jews said: "See how he loved Lazarus!" Rather I think: "See how he loved her." He was moved to tears of compassion for one He loved who suffered so deeply. "Show me where he lies," Jesus said. They did. Jesus called out, and Lazarus came forth. One can only begin to imagine the unmitigated joy of these two loving women as Jesus handed Lazarus over to them that day.

This morning we can take comfort from this Scripture. Jesus understands our pain. He wants us to be consoled in the face of this pain of loss. Br. Vincent has left our midst, but we are assured that he has gone to a better life, everlasting life. It is not for us to know if he will play his saxophone there, or take up his masonry tools or use any of the marvelous practical skills he had honed over the years. What we do know, and Jesus assures us, Br. Vincent is destined for eternal life. "Eye has not seen, nor ear heard, nor have entered into the heart of man the things which God has prepared for those who love him." (1 Cor. 2:9) We can easily imagine Jesus, the carpenter, saying: "Well done, good and faithful servant."

I would like to add a small personal comment. I found it so touching and significant that Richard Niehaus, his coworker and devoted friend, was at his bedside when Br. Vincent died. Richard, unwittingly, became a symbol for all other co-workers and friends whose lives Br. Vincent touched over the years.

Now we must let go and move on. We honor him by believing he is with God. We honor him by facing our world with faith. We honor Br. Vincent when we model our lives on the faith-filled way he lived his life and faced his death.

May he rest in peace.

Br. Lawrence Shidler, O.S.B.

Reflection prepared for the memorial service for Br. Lawrence, April 12, 2004.

On behalf of Fr. Archabbot and the community, I express my sincere condolences to the family of Br. Lawrence and of his brother, Leo, who died on the same day as Br. Lawrence. Your family has had a heavy burden these days. Br. Lawrence was always deeply committed to his family. Although he would allow that he came from humble beginnings, they were beginnings in a saintly family with holy and faith-filled parents—a grace no money could buy. You family members, here for this funeral, will attest to that. Your parents may not have been able to endow a chair, but they left a legacy of faith and love that continues to pay out in our midst. Mourn him, family and friends, weep for his passing, but never doubt for a moment that he was a holy man and is now with God.

Br. Lawrence was the senior brother in the community. He enrolled at St. Placid Hall when he was 15 in 1935. He entered the novitiate in 1938 and made his first vows in 1939. Although others had come to the monastery before Br. Lawrence and Br. Benedict from St. Placid Hall, those two very soon were the seniors of that pioneer group that initiated the junior brothers program. Until that time, the ethos of the monastery was German. Prayers, table reading and conversation were all in German. Beginnings are hard. One can only guess now how difficult it must have been to carve a niche for the English-speaking brothers in a very entrenched community. No one would call Br. Lawrence an innovator, but his stability, dedication and obedience made him a model leader for all who have come after to this day. Even in his old age, with very little to say, he spoke loudly by the example of his monastic observance.

"Little to say," embodies much of what we might say about Br. Lawrence. Talkative he was not. Keeping silence was not one of his heaviest burdens, and inane conversation was not one of his faults. With a voice that barely rose above a whisper, except perhaps at the card table, he went around in his quiet way, yet never aloof from the community.

He was a very private man and expressed himself softly without hugs and embraces. Nonetheless, he was loving, and blest were those who managed to get beyond the gates. I remember with particular delight one time when I asked him something about the mechanism of the pendulum clock. He became animated and went on and on. I confess I was paying more attention to the fact that he was so loquacious than to the information he was providing. His face had lighted up like a flower in the morning light.

It is only fair to say, and I think it needs to be said, that Br. Lawrence was a very pious man. Not in a superficial or saccharine way, but in that deep response to God's call in the ordinariness of everyday life. Unknown to many, he spent time each day before the Blessed Sacrament, he was faithful to the Divine Office, and he served the brethren with unselfish love. To say that he was steady would belabor the obvious. He was a rock of stability, and his brothers in the community knew that and respected it.

I mentioned his card playing. One saw another side of Br. Lawrence at the card table and, earlier, on the handball court. If anyone ever thought him a Milquetoast, they had not met him at the card table or on any sports field. He was a very good athlete and continued to play handball well into his 70s. Let's just say he did not take losing lightly. He seldom had to.

If there was a proud bone in his body, it might have been over his carpentry skills. He had apprenticed in carpentry from the earliest days of his coming to Saint Meinrad. Like everybody else who went to work there, he began by sweeping the floor of wood chips and sawdust, but he soon moved into becoming a most skilled artisan. There has been practically no carpentry job in the community that he has not been involved with in some way for the past 50 years. He was on his way to work when he suffered his injuries that contributed to his death. Over all these years, he prepared the coffins that the monks would be buried in, always keeping at least one on hand. One never knows. The coffin you made for others may be the one for you.

Most of his skilled labor is hidden around the Hill. There is no signature on his work. Its art is in its function. The wood products on the Hill are witness to his artistry. Of special interest though, is Brother's crafting of crosiers. Bishops and abbots from around the country attest to the beauty of the staffs he has provided them over the years, even the crosier of his cousin Bishop Gettlefinger of the Diocese of Evansville, and I dare say it will be used tomorrow at the funeral Mass, as Bishop Gettlefinger presides. One such crosier sits permanently at Fr. Archabbot's choir stall, and others are used in various ceremonies. For decades, he has crafted chalices and matching communion bowls. One could go on and on. After all, he was a carpenter for over 60 years!

He was our watch repairman for over 40 years. I really do not know when he started, but I know that he inherited the watchmaker's tools from Br. Alphonse Veith, who died in 1956. I am sure that he never attended a workshop or had training of any kind, but he could almost always get the watch back in your hands, running, in a timely manner. I know of at least four clocks that he kept running on time, winding and resetting them once a week or more for the past 20 years at least. Unfortunately, he did not have an apprentice. It will be interesting to see how the clocks survive his passing. I have checked. They are all still running, but they have lost or gained time and, unless attended to, will soon stop altogether.

In like manner, just this past week Br. Jonah, Br. Lawrence's young assistant in the carpenter shop, had to provide the wood and prepare the fire for Holy Saturday, a task Br. Lawrence had routinely taken care of for over 30 years.

I will miss him. I will miss his quiet presence almost haunting the halls of the monastery. I will miss his smile that would transform his face from grim to radiant joy in the time it took to say hello. I am sure you will miss him, too, but we must let him go. He has fought the good fight and now it is time for God to receive this good and faithful servant. May he rest in peace.

Homily for the Funeral Mass of Fr. Rembert Gehant, O.S.B

The Gospel reading for the funeral Mass was from Luke 7:11-15

Let me offer words of consolation to the family and friends of Fr. Rembert. Thank you for joining us this morning to lay our Brother to rest. One of the downsides of living so long is that there are few left to mourn your passing. We in the community here are in a better position to appreciate his many qualities, as a person and as a monk, because we have lived with him for so many years. Father was the second oldest among us. There are seven monks professed longer than he, but only one who is older, Fr. Theodore. Be consoled that Fr. Rembert lived and died among his monk-brothers. He never regretted the vocational call he responded to with such generosity.

The short Gospel passage from Luke reveals Jesus' encounter with the widow of Naim just outside the gates of that little village. They are only a few words, but they offer an eternity of hope. We could put together a chain of passages showing the deep compassion of Jesus, and His great power, even over death itself. Ours is a short passage. It tells how Jesus, out of compassion, raised the young son, her only son, being carried to his burial. Jesus restored him to his mother.

Three times the Gospels report Jesus' restoration of life to a dead person. There is this son of the widow of Naim. There is the raising of the daughter of Jairus, and the calling forth from the tomb of Lazarus, the brother of Martha and Mary. Only in our passage is the relative for whom the miracle was performed unknown. Jesus, in each case, was moved with compassion for the living. It is that compassion we call upon today, not that He should restore physical life to Fr. Rembert, but that He will raise him up to a high place in heaven. The story of the raising of the son of the widow of Naim is told in only a few words, but an eternity of hope is given in the story of the compassion of Jesus.

We are confronted with death again this morning, death that stalks our every step. It behooves us, as St. Benedict says, to keep death daily before our eyes. As surely as Fr. Rembert watched and waited, we are watching and waiting for our hour. Step by small step, minute by minute, we are closing in on death, and we need to move along, sure-footed, to the great mysteries that await us. We can approach death with confidence and hope because of the teaching of Jesus. Fr. Rembert's death and burial confronts us with the reality that, like him, we, too, will die and be buried. What we are at that moment will depend very much on how we live this moment and all the moments still at our disposal.

For Fr. Rembert, death came only after years of preparation. For him, the progression was slow, as age dug into his body, and of late, his mind. In a way, it was sad to watch this stripping away of humanity, but it was his lot and will be for most of us. We do well to prepare our hearts for these coming events and to deepen our faith in the verities that underlie it. Such faith is the foundation of our hope.

Fr. Rembert was quintessentially a quiet man. Who else would press his forefinger against his upper lip to hold back laughter like it was a sneeze? He seldom raised his voice. If he was quiet, and he was, he could blow you away with his occasional comments. At times, this meek and quiet man was a flaming liberal. He obviously thought deeply about his faith. Not infrequently, he probed deeper than more faint-hearted would dare to go. He was not obsessed by issues of the hour, though he could speak of them. He could and did turn his mind to sports, politics and news of the day with ease and zest. He lived his life with an intensity of dedication. He was always where he should be at the appointed times. His life was a model for us, his brothers and, in the larger scheme of things, for the world. He was a quiet man, but the example of his life was a shout before the throne of God, surely heard in the heavens and in its muffled tones in each of us.

It so happened that I was with Father when he died. Sad as it was, it was a lovely moment. Br. Paul and Novice Arthur were also there. We like to think we saw his lips move in prayer as we prayed aloud at his bedside. We called on Mary to pray for us sinners now and at the hour of our death. I am sure she did. Perhaps a little off tune, but with touched hearts, we sang the "Salve" calling upon our sweet Mother to be mindful of him and of us all. May he rest in peace.

The Discovery of a Manuscript

*The following little bit of whimsy was written in Rome during a sabbatical in 1984.
It is a tongue-in-cheek jab at academia and highlights a librarian's obsession with lost
books.*

Only by chance did I come across the Latin manuscript that has so absorbed my
energies in recent years. A semester sabbatical had provided the opportunity for
personal study. I was engaged in reviewing the collaborative work of Adelbert
deVogue, OSB, and Ambrose Wathen, OSB, on the Rule of the Master and the
Rule of Benedict, when I happened on a non-titled work, apparently by a librarian, on dealing with delinquent library users. I have gathered here notes published individually elsewhere in small library and literary journals. They are
reprinted here as they first appeared, except in a few instances where revisions
have been made in the light of later conclusions.

Rare Ms. Uncovered

Cf. Kent State Library Notes v. 72 (1942)

In 1967, pursuing a research project on the Rule of the Master and its relation to
the Rule of Benedict, I came across a hitherto unknown and unlisted manuscript.
In codex Paris. B.N.L. 12634 I found this fascicle between leaves 150v. and 151r.
(hereafter referred to as *Pro Preservatione).* Lowe, in his monumental work on
Latin manuscripts (Lowe, E. A. (Elias Avery), 1879-1969. *Palaeographical papers,*
1907-1965; edited by Ludwig Bieler, 1972 2v.), seems either to have missed it
entirely, or purposely failed any mention of it because it is so obviously an inser-
tion in the Codex. The Codex in which *Pro Preservatione* is found dates from the
9th century, but our manuscript seems to be in a much later hand, from the 14th
or 15th century.

The problem of dating a particular manuscript, even within a codex, is ever a
critical concern. All too frequently, all the manuscript within a codex are assumed
to be of the same date as the first one that has been studied and dated. The folly
of this practice was highlighted in 1935 by Jean Destrez *La pecia dans les*

manuscrits universitares du XIIIe et du XIVe siècle. Therein he showed that individual fascicles (pescia) within a codex might be of different hands, from different families, and/or written at different times and places. In any case, our manuscript, *Pro Preservatione*, is not of the 9th century, though all the other manuscripts of BNL12634 do date from that period. Lowe may have skipped our manuscript out of concern for its dating, etc., or it is just possible that his entry for BNL 12634 depended on the indexing of an earlier source that had ignored it.

Since my original discovery of *Pro Preservatione*, I have found two other manuscripts of this work, one in Italian and the other also in Latin. Each was found, unindexed and tipped in. However, they were both in codices having other monastic writings. I am convinced that the original was in Latin and that the one in Italian is a translation. This conclusion is based on internal evidence. Just as an example, the phrase *movimento duro* occurs several times in the Italian in places where it was difficult to make any sense of the Latin passage. Later when I found the second Latin manuscript, I discovered some glosses had been added in English, one of which is "tough s—t." The Italian translator obviously didn't understand, but he showed some imagination in his translation. The question remains open, but until more evidence is found, we will presume the original was written in Latin.

About the Author

I will report the conclusions of my study on the author of *Pro Preservatione* and follow with some data from which my judgment was made.

I say the author is Joannes Trithemius, OSB, known and revered as Abbot Trithemius (John Trithemius), a famous scholar and Benedictine abbot, born at Trittenheim on the Moselle, 1 February, 1462; died at Würzburg, 13 December, 1516. He was a monk of Sponheim and, after his retirement, of Würzburg, a Scottish monastery. *Pro Preservatione* was probably written in 1514. The English glosses on one Latin manuscript were added by one Eberhard, a librarian of Würtzburg and living around the same period. There seems to be little purpose in seeking an earlier author since the lending of books and manuscripts was very rare. Richard de Bury, a contemporary of Trithemius, also seems to have had quite a collection of books. He conceivably could have written our essay, but if the scuttlebutt of the English Benedictine communities can be trusted, he probably stole many of his books. That being the case, he would hardly have expressed these notions even if he had them, though his great distain for library users is reflected in his Philobiblion, where he speaks of sniffling readers.

A study of the unpublished *Chronica Wurzburgensis* reveals that Trithemius was kind of obsessed by the disappearance of books from his library, which was probably one of the most prestigious libraries on the continent at the time. The *Catholic Encyclopedia* (1904) has this to say about Trithemius:

"Although he was the youngest member of the community, and had not yet been ordained, he was elected abbot at the age of 22, during the second year of his life in the order. His election was a great blessing for Sponheim. With youthful vigor and a firm hand, he undertook the direction of the much-neglected monastery. He first turned his attention to the material needs of his community, then set himself to the much more difficult task of restoring its discipline. Above all, his own example, not only in the conscientious observance of the rules of the order, but also in the tireless pursuit of scientific studies, brought about the happiest results.

"In order to promote effectively scientific research, he procured a rich collection of books which comprised the most important works in all branches of human knowledge; in this way he built up the world-renowned library of Sponheim for the enriching of which he labored unceasingly for 23 years till the collection numbered about 2,000 volumes. This library, unique in those days, made Sponheim known throughout the entire world of learning. The attractive personality of the abbot also helped to spread the fame of the monastery. Among his friends he numbered not only the most learned men of his time, such as Conrad Celtes, Johannes Reuchlin, and John of Dalberg, but also many princes—including the Emperor Maximilian, who held him in great esteem. But the farther his reputation extended in the world, the greater became the number of malcontents in the monastery who opposed the abbot's discipline. Finally, he resigned as head of his beloved abbey, which he had ruled for 23 years, and which he had brought to a most flourishing condition. After his departure, the monastery sank into its former insignificance...

"Trithemius sought the quiet and peace of a more retired life, and this he found as abbot of the Scottish monastery of St. Jacob, at Würzburg (1506). Here he found only three monks, so he had ample opportunity to display the same activity he had shown at Sponheim. He spent the last ten years of his life in the production of many important writings. Only once did he leave his monastery (1508), for a short stay at the imperial court. He died at 55 years of age and was buried in the Scottish church at Würzburg."

"The great abbot," says one of his biographers, "was equally worthy of respect as a man, as a religious, and as a writer." Of his more than 80 works, only part have appeared in print. The greater number of these are ascetical writings, which treat the religious life and were published by John Busaeus, S.J., under the title *Joannis Trithemii opera pia et spiritualia* (Mainz, 1604); they are among the best works of devotional literature produced at the time."

More conclusive for me, though, are the references in *Chronica Wrzburgensis* mentioned above. And the fact that in the year 1514, Trithemius is reported to have bladder problems and possibly prostate cancer. I came on this fact in the *Chronica* after I had noticed a high occurrence of p in a literary analysis of the text. There were 302 p's in this short text, 40 of which are doubled. That is a standard deviation of ten over the normal doubling of letters. That pp was an abbreviation for urination cannot be determined from standard dictionaries, but it is listed in Blackstern's *Medaeival Argot in Northern England in the 15ᵗʰ Century*. It is reasonable to conclude that the high incidence of pp in the text is significant and points to a person preoccupied with problems of the urinary tract. Trithemius is our man.

On the basis of the same evidence, I date the manuscript from the period of 1510-1516, pinpointing as closely as I can to 1514. I know that some will find fault with my use of this evidence, but I am so convinced of the correctness of my judgment in this matter that I am tempted to quote Eberhard, whose interjection loses something in Italian translation.

Prophesy or Insight:
A Study and Translation of a Text

Anyone reading today Joannes Trithemius' tirade against book thieves, as below translated, would be tempted to believe it is a late 20ᵗʰ-century document. There is a kind of transcendence here in the ideas expressed, born of a seething fury. Librarians even today struggle, on the one hand, to cope with their own anger and yet to continue to find some way to address the problem. Trithemius didn't mince words. I have tried to preserve their force in translation without some of its crudity. (What does one do with *contundit testiculos eorum*?) I have translated *certa res*, literally a certain thing, as a chip, and *machina* (machine) as a computer, since in our days the generic thing he describes can thus be expressed in specific terms.

I do not ascribe theological prophecy to this tract. What I think we have here is an insight, born of anguish and suffering, that empowered him to new heights of meanness and oppression, and an imaginative insight for the solution. Only in our day has the technology, both hardware and software, become available.

This tract may never have been meant for distribution. Many of his other manuscripts remain unpublished. This piece lacks the usual greetings, salutations and conclusions. The theological problem it posed and the fact that at that time there were no physical means to accomplish his plans are reasons enough to explain its lack of popularity. If the negotiations with IBM for hardware and the written agreement I have with OCLC for software is any indication, this plan has great potential in our times.

This rough draft of musings could be developed into cross-disciplinary studies involving library science, electronics, chemistry, moral theology, computer technology, and medicine, to name a few. Once in place and operative, this system should provide a rich market for the legal profession. Here follows my translation of the text, using the two Latin editions and the Italian translation.

Plans for a Security System for Libraries With Options

(By Joannes Trithemius)

I propose an electronic security system for the preservation of book collections that plays on fears natural to man—there are options for getting women.

The first proposal deals with the implantation in every book of a gadget (read chip), miniaturized, of course, that can be remotely activated. It will be the nature of this device that once activated it will give off rays that attack the gonads of the possessor, rendering him sterile for life. Presumably, it would be possible to temper this process so the full effect would apply only when the abuse is flagrant.

A more mitigated approach, one available for women users and perhaps as an earlier stage for men offenders, would be a device capable of generating a foul odor sufficient to permeate in a quasi-permanent manner the immediate environs of the ill-gotten or overlong-held book.

Books for which there is a circulation card made out, the date due would determine the time for activation of these devices. Some period of grace might be allowed, depending on the disposition of the librarian at the time. Justice dictating—or at least allowing—activation on the date due; charity pressing for a day or two of grace.

To reach their full potential as a deterrent, public notices should clearly point out the dangers and duly play upon fears that might normally be consequent to such information.

Until such devices are on the market and duly tested (theologians are presently discussing whether the principle of the double effect is applicable for test volunteers or for a man eager for sterilization, who purposely keeps a book overdue), a chip might be used on which were recorded screams of women that would be repeated at intervals of one half hour until deactivated in the library. For women, there would be chips on which heavy breathing or perhaps a recording of the sounds of mice at play could be activated. Both these devices could be put in every book, but only that one activated which seems most appropriate.

I conceive of another chip that might, when activated, send an electronic message to a computer that records the information about the holder and the book for possible printout for police. This information would be immediately fed to another computer that would call the party offending at half-hour intervals until a counter message is received from the librarian.

These measures, so far briefly described, are for books duly charged out. More drastic surprises are in store for those who, falsely hoping to bypass dire consequences, dare to remove a book without charging it out. Present planning includes generating an electronic field in the library with a device in every book that must be duly discharged or it will emit earsplitting electronic noises if it leaves the field uncharged.

A more drastic variation of this, discussed here more for theory than practice, would have an item removed without being charged out explode when it leaves the electronic field. It may be presumed that in the beginning the library might lose a few items to this destructive force. However, the consequent maiming of a few, it is believed, would tend, presumably for a good number of years, though minimally for a school year, to eliminate all attempts at theft.

To prevent blood being splattered all over the library, a 30-second interval could be built into the device before it detonates, after leaving the electromagnetic field of the library building.

It may be of interest to note that moral principles are being developed, according to the needs of the time, to support such programs. An analogous principle to the moral dictum, *caveat emptor,* i.e. "let the buyer beware," is "let the borrower beware." According to this principle, every borrower will have been duly warned of dire consequences, and thus as a moral person assumes full responsibility for the consequences of his delinquency. The principle not to kill is an absolute, but it can be argued that maiming is *de minimis* and, permissible, at least to contemplate for the common good. One may have to derive principles based on a Muslim morality to ground this practice more soundly.

Another principle, analogous to a Gospel dictum, is that "one book can be destroyed to save the many." The fact that a hand is lost then would fall under the principle of the double effect. There does seem to be some foundation for such a principle, but spelling it out takes us down roads too far afield for this proposal. I long for the day when book collections can be safeguarded, even as they are allowed to be used by others.

The Roman Experience:
A Strange Interlude

In the spring of 1984, I enjoyed a sabbatical semester in Rome, most of it in the company of Fr. Rupert. I was there a little longer than he and, in the early stages of my travels, I visited Maresous Abbey in Belgium. I had made the acquaintance of Br. Ferdinand Poswick, O.S.B., a computer expert, who had visited Saint Meinrad. Br. Ferdinand was vitally interested in seeing the European Catholic libraries move to automation. He had access to a rather powerful computer.

There were special problems over and above the learning, equipping and financing such a project. Not least of them was the telephone system or the variety and lack of dependability of such services throughout Europe. He hoped to bypass that problem by creating the database of all the Catholic libraries on his computer, from which he would distribute the database to individual institutions on CD-ROM. This would give each library access to the whole database without having to use phone lines.

It was an interesting concept and I enjoyed talking with him and sharing with him more details of the automation available in the USA through OCLC. It so happened that he was scheduled to have a workshop for the Pontifical University libraries of Rome at a time when I would be in there. He asked me to appear for one session and explain to the librarians of Rome what we were doing in the States. The workshop he was conducting was an effort to convince a reluctant group that there was an economy of scale that could come from a union catalog and that patrons could be much better served with such a system.

I made my presentation in English. Most of them understood and there were translators to help the others. I was shown some deference and my talk aroused the interest of a number of them. One man, who was head of the Vatican School of Library Science, Mr. Ivan Rebernik, arranged for me to have a personal tour of the Vatican Library at another time.

After the tour, we sat for a while in his office. He told a rather sad tale of woe over staffing and the almost hopeless attitude of staff toward automation. He explained that there were men working in the library with absolutely no interest or enthusiasm and who neglected their work, but were untouchable because of family connections with cardinals. It was sad. He seemed very competent and dedicated to the library. His sadness at his situation pervaded the interview.

As I was about to leave, he got very serious and asked me to consider becoming the Vatican librarian for printed books. He did not expect an immediate answer. He kept insisting we needed only a few honest and dedicated men, possibly having to work around the deadbeats. He assured me that he would help in any way he could. This had nothing to do with automation. That might come. Before anything, though, he wanted a good administrator. It seems the present librarian, a good and dedicated Monsignor Paul Carnart, whom I later met, wanted desperately to get back to the manuscript department that he had headed up before the librarian job came open and needed to be filled.

I explained to Ivan, as best I could, that I was in no position to give an answer. Even if I wanted the job, my superior would have to give approval. For his part, he said he understood that and added my application for the job had to be submitted to the cardinal prefect of the library. He asked me to prepare a brief *curriculum vitae*, so that he would have something to show the cardinal prefect. As you might imagine, I left the environs in a dither.

I am a little fuzzy on the sequence of events that followed. All together, I was engaged for several weeks with these negotiations. I prepared my *curriculum vitae* and gave it to him. It was handwritten because I did not have benefit of a typewriter. It wasn't but a few days later that Ivan called to say that he had presented his proposal to the cardinal prefect, who, without a lot of discussion, said no to the plan. He did not want an American.

Truthfully, I was relieved. I had a vague notion I might be able to bring some better procedures to the library, but the task would have been daunting. I asked for a secretary, but was told that only the prefect has a secretary. There was one circa 1930 manual typewriter in the library. No word processors or other electronic systems. At home, I had just moved into a beautiful new library building with automation well on the way, and a personal computer for my own use. To walk away from all that, at the age of 62, and start over was a big order, and gave me great pause. Ivan had played on my emotions by insisting I had a responsibility to the Church to step up in this time of emergency. I got around to deciding that I was willing to make the sacrifice. Happily, it was not required.

Of course, I was sending out one letter after the other to Fr. Archabbot, apprising him of what was going on, but at the time had no word back. I informed him that the deal was off. Then I got a call from Ivan asking me to have dinner with him and Msgr. Canart at some nearby restaurant. In my mind, it was to be a happy conclusion to all the turmoil I had been through.

Well into the meal, they made a new proposal, that I become the coordinator of the joint library project planned by the twelve or so Pontifical Libraries of Rome. Although it was still in the talking stage, these men were convinced that automation was the way to go, and that someone with some experience would have to stay on top of it to make the project succeed. This was not a field of expertise for me, though I had had considerable experience in being a participant in the formation of the Indiana Cooperative Library Services Authority, which among other things brokered automation for the Indiana libraries. I was back in the stew.

These two men, who were key figures on the Vatican library scene, were railroading a deal that the other libraries had not agreed to. An automated union catalog had been discussed, but there was no unanimity among the group for how it should be done. If I remember correctly, only two or three of the libraries had any automation. They crossed a line for me when they insisted that I open an office right away. They tried to assure me that they would get the necessary permissions. I was somewhat resigned to the possibility, but insisted that I return home as planned at the end of the semester. Then do a lot of consulting before any thought of returning.

Of course, somewhat embarrassed, I had to write to the abbot again. He solved the problem categorically by saying I was needed at home. Obedience was never so sweet. That I can recall. We never spoke of it again. I had the feeling that Fr. Abbot felt I was angling to stay in Rome. In my heart, nothing could be further from the truth. It was such a brief interlude in my life. Nothing ever came of it, and very few people know that I was once, for whatever reasons, offered the job of Vatican Librarian, Printed Books Section.

As a footnote, I can say that the job of Vatican Librarian went to an Irish Dominican, a medievalist, well respected in the academic world, Fr. Leonard Boyle. He was able to accomplish much of what we few dreamers could only hope for. He made several trips to the States and was as nearby as Louisville, though I never met the man. Today there is an automated union catalog of Roman theological libraries. Fr. Boyle passed away not too long after he was encouraged to resign because his superiors in the Vatican did not approve of some of the ways he was raising money for projects. However, he had managed to bring the library out of the doldrums and once again take its place as one of the premier libraries of the world.

Kind Words for Cordelia

I had a nice moment the other day. Although it was of my own doing, I hope that it was also a nice moment for Cordelia. I had every indication that it was.

"Cordelia" is really Ms. Martha Powell, currently catalog librarian, but formerly music librarian at Southern Baptist Theological Seminary in Louisville, KY. I met Martha in connection with my library work.

One summer in the early 1970s, Ron Deering, librarian of Southern Baptist Seminary in Louisville, KY, invited me to join him and two of his staff in the car trip to Toronto, Canada, to attend the annual meeting of the American Theological Library Association being held there. Martha was one of the staff members who went for that ride.

Because we had all looked forward to a planned outing to a nearby town and a Shakespearean theater, I thought it fitting that we familiarize ourselves with the text of "King Lear" by reading it during the long stretches of automobile travel. I provided copies. We divided the characters among us and read the play through from beginning to end. In the story, as most know, Cordelia is the beloved daughter of King Lear, his only hope and consolation in the world in which he comes to a tragic end. Martha read the female parts. She was Cordelia to "my" Lear.

From that time on, I spoke to and of Martha as Cordelia, truth to tell, Sweet Cordelia. It was an inside joke between us and it persisted down the years.

In 1994, another librarian friend, Nancy Robinson, called for testimonials for Martha, which she would then have bound into a book that could be given to her. The occasion was Martha's 25 years of library service at the Southern Baptist Seminary.

For reasons unexplained, I did not get my copy off by the deadline Nancy had given, and I feared my words would not be included with the others.

In the process of cleaning out files, I came across a carbon of my words. I was prepared to discard them, as so many other memories have been swept away. Actually, I was touched by what I read and wondered to myself what was going on in Martha's life, now these ten years later. I had presumed that she had left library work and moved to either Texas or Wyoming. I called the SBTS library to see if I could get her address. I learned that she was still with the library and was available. We talked for some time about old times and then I had the opportunity to reread my testimonial to her firsthand. I was in tears by the time I finished. It became one more precious moment, filled with grace, which has so enriched my life. She, for her part, seemed deeply touched.

(Before reading the letter, I would like to add a brief note that may belabor the obvious, but knowing the background enhances the power of the letter I think. I coined the word "Cyranesque." That refers to a character in a play by Edmond Rostand titled *Cyrano de Bergerac*. Briefly, Cyrano is a symbol of an unrequited lover. In the play, Cyrano, because of his grotesquely large nose "that marches on/before me by a quarter of an hour," is convinced that he is too ugly to deserve his adored Roxane. Cyrano helps his inarticulate rival, Christian, win her heart by allowing him to present Cyrano's love poems, speeches, and letters as his own work. Soon the romance starts; Christian whispers his own love from the shadows in glorious words that Roxane believes are his. But Christian realizes that it was not his own good looks but Cyrano's letters that won Roxanne. Before his death on the battlefield, Christian asks Cyrano to confess their plot to Roxane. Cyrano keeps their secret for fourteen years. She, in grief over the death of her young spouse, had retired to a convent where Cyrano came to visit her once a week for 14 years. He would tell her the news of the hour and describe to her his exploits of the week. Badly beaten, bleeding, he visits her one last time. Here he does reveal the truth: "That night when 'neath your window Christian spoke/—Under your balcony, you remember? Well!/There was the allegory of my whole life:/I, in the shadow, at the ladder's foot,/While others lightly mount to Love and Fame!" It dawns on her that it was really Cyrano whose love had stirred her so, through all the years. Cyrano dies with his head in her lap.)

Dear Martha,

Comes now, late, my testimony. Late by fault, but late fortuitously because my words do not belong among those of people you have worked closely with over the years. Not that my words are any less sincere. I come not as a student, nor as a teacher. I have never heard you play the piano or organ or heard you sing. I have seldom spent more than ten or 20 minutes in your presence at a time. You just have to plan a little space at the end of the book of testimonials for words from a friend and colleague who admires your beauty of body and soul and who has borne witness to his love and respect by one or two visits a year for most of the 25 years you are celebrating. My "ad limina" visits are Cyranesque, as I recount the news of the hour, trusting that some time before the last one you will recognize the devotion that underlies the report.

I hope that this note may warm your heart. As the years go by and you reread it, perhaps long after I have gone, I hope that you will remember warmly the one who called you "Cordelia," made his "ad limina" visits, and kept you up on the news of the hour several times each year.

The Mysterious Key

After I have been laid to rest and my few possessions get dispersed, my keys will be turned in to the locksmith. He will be in for a little surprise when he finds one of them does not fit any lock on the Hill. What possibly could possess a man to carry a key that opens nothing? Where in the world was the lock for which it was made? And why in the world would he carry it around, perhaps for years?

Well, now it can be said. It opens the door to the home of a friend who lives in Texas. Perhaps she was the lone and silent figure, in black, skirting the edges of the funeral procession at my burial. She might just show up then, somewhat in reparation for not having come before.

It was late 2000 or early 2001 that I had occasion to visit her in her home. (I have known her for all of 30 years.) Since she had to be at work most of the day, she provided me with the key to her front door so that I could come and go throughout the day. By mistake, I went off without returning it, and when I offered to mail it, she suggested I keep it just in case I should ever return.

In the ordinary course of my daily life, I have occasion to use my keys at least three times. Thus, I encounter it there on my key ring day in and day out. Each time, I have a little something to say to her, so my memory of her and her friendship is ever alive.

As the locksmith ponders this mysterious key that opens nothing in the area, he will note that there is no key to my cell on the ring. Oops! It wasn't lost, but shipped off to Texas in hopes said lady may take a similar opportunity to keep my memory ever in mind. It dawned on me to do that a short time after I had initiated the practice of taking note of the key day by day.

Truth to tell, there was a minor crisis when I was told I had to leave the cell that I had lived in for 20 years. Naturally, I was asked to turn in my key. In a minor panic, I assured the locksmith that I would locate it in due time. Hastily, I insisted that my friend return the key, which she did. Then I promptly sent her the key to my new cell at her request. Well, at least with her consent. I do not think it is as big a deal with her as it is for me. Of course, she will never use it, except as a reminder of her friend far, far away.

I am a sentimental old man. I am deeply touched by the people who have showered me with love over the years. That love has enriched my life. I treasure this little reminder of an ongoing friendship and I make no apology for carrying around this mysterious key that opens nothing but the door of my heart.

See this little key.
It is dear to me.
It goes wherever I go.

It opens and closes
A distant door.
But even more
It opens and closes my heart,
And nurtures a friendship
And love, which for my part,
Are also very dear to me.

Each day and throughout the day
As I finger the ring that holds the key,
I have occasion to address the one
Behind the door that it fits,
Trusting that by some mysterious way
She may receive my greeting and respond.

It does seem a bit odd
For a monk in vows
To hold such a token,
But token it is
Of a legitimate love
That continues to enrich my life.

"Good morning,"
I say.
Or "Good evening, dear one,"
And then go on.

No harm done.
In some way I hope
To touch her heart
As she has touched mine
And keep alive
The chaste loves that bind.

So I will go on
Carrying this key
That opens my heart.
I will go on
Mumbling my greetings.

Mayhaps in another part of the world
She might get the message,
And share the joy,
And feel support
From a love expressed
So far away.

A Campus Walk in September

Whether this walk ever took place, I am not sure. It could have. It is a little story that was told me many years ago. I do not remember by whom. It describes a very likely scene. That September evening was far enough back that there was no air-conditioning on the Hill. Evening Compline, chanted by the monks in the Abbey Church, could be heard wafting across the valley through the open windows.

Two new students, who had arrived on campus only a few days before, were on an evening stroll in front of the Major Seminary buildings. As they walked and talked, they could not help but be distracted by the new sights and sounds around them.

At one point in their walk, almost as if by cue, they stopped in their tracks and looked at each other in a kind of awe. One of them, listening to the sounds of the voices of the monks, said: "Isn't that beautiful!"

The other young man, whose ear was more attuned to nature, was listening to the crickets and he said: "Yeah, and to think that they do that by rubbing their legs together."

Gören Ogén

He had a hard time saying "thistle," I remember. His native language was Swedish, but he did tolerably well in English, and German, and Spanish, and French, and Latin. He was a good person to have around when traveling. I was traveling that fall of 1967. I was on an informally planned tour of Benedictine abbeys in Europe. I had a new Volkswagen sedan and was well into my trip when I met him at Pierre-qui-Vire in central France.

I was 45 years old at the time and on my first sabbatical leave from my work in the Saint Meinrad Archabbey Library, where I had served as librarian since August of 1951. I left Saint Meinrad in May. It was November when I met Gören. I planned to head south to EnCalcat near the Spanish border, but before I would arrive there, I wanted to visit Taize, an ecumenical monastery in Central France that I had heard so much about.

Gören was 19 years old, also on somewhat of a sabbatical from studies, having completed his studies before entering the university. He was a convert to Catholicism and had spent a good bit of time at the Abbey of Clervaux in Luxemburg. While there, he had met up with and did some work for Fr. Jean LeClercq, a world-renowned scholar in the area of Benedictine monasticism. Fr. Jean, in response to Gören's request, made contact with a number of Benedictine guest masters so that he would be welcomed as he worked his way south to spend the winter months as leisurely as he could on the shores of the Mediterranean.

His time at Pierre-qui-Vire was very unromantic. He was assigned heavy work on the construction site for a new abbey church. The weather was cold and damp. He was spending most of his free moments in bed, to both rest and keep warm. This was hardly what he was looking for. He spoke to the guest master who, in turn, spoke to me and we agreed that he could travel with me to the next site further south even though it would take us a few days to get there. And so the saga began. What started out to be a quasi-taxi ride ended up being a trip that extended over a month.

He was a delightful traveling companion. He was fresh and vivacious, interested and intelligent and his language skills came in handy all along the way. I had lucked out and he seemed happy enough to continue on with me, even though it altered all the plans he had made for the year. He ended up returning to Lund when my travels were over.

In the meantime, we visited Taize, EnCalcat, San Michel de Cuxa and Lourdes in France. Montserrat in Spain. San Anselmo and San Gerolimo in Rome. At that point, he had connected with Fr. Jean LeClerq, who promised to help him get into monasteries in the south of Italy. In a sense, that was our good-bye. I remember carrying his suitcase up to the entrance of the monastery. I embraced him as he stepped across the threshold and presumably out of my life. I felt like a father leaving his son at the door of a monastery. I turned and left, quietly crying within. We had had such a lovely time together that it was hard to part.

Imagine my surprise a few days later as I was entering the church at San Anselmo with the community there, when I saw him. I got out of line and rushed to him, afraid that something was wrong. He told me that he had decided to cut his trip short and asked if he could accompany me as far as Heidelberg in Germany, where I was headed. Needless to say, I was delighted. We had another few days together as we proceeded north through Italy, Switzerland, Austria and Germany.

Toward the end of our journey, Gören became more introspective, as he seemed to be wrestling with personal decisions. Finally, in a brief conversation, he told me he had made three resolutions: 1) To pursue a doctorate in the psychology of religion, 2) To marry Arline, an American exchange student he had met at school in Lund. I do not believe that they had ever dated, but she left a precious love note in his locker the day she left for America. 3) If he ever had a boy, he would name him Simeon. It turned out that he carried out all three of his resolutions.

He got a degree in the psychology of religion from a prestigious institute in Zurich, after a good number of years of work and study.

He came to the States in the summer of 1968 and proposed to Arline. She accepted, but insisted on finishing her college program before marriage. She had three years to go. He agreed to wait. She, in the meantime, took instruction in the Catholic Church and was baptized at least conditionally, before they were married.

I visited them in their home in Lund, Sweden, in 1976. They had two lovely little girls. I returned again in 1984 and there was the six-year-old Simeon Ogen. I was proud as a peacock!

I was fortunate enough to have a final opportunity to visit Gören and his family for a week in January of 2000. We had both changed a lot over the years, but there was and is a bond between us that is precious to me. I have only fond memories of the month we were together and will always treasure that time.

I met Gören at a special time in my life. I grew up a lot in the months I was in Europe in 1967. I was already 45 years old, but had never been on my own before. It was wonderfully reassuring to learn that I had the tools, intellectually and emotionally, to cope with many different situations with confidence. Some of the encounters I had on that trip enriched my life and continue to do so. As precious as almost any of them was the bond that developed between Gören and me. I have never before or since felt so much like a father with his son. Even as I write this, close to my 82nd birthday, I am looking forward to a visit from Simeon Ogen, Goren's only son. I am still full of loving memories of Simeon's father's time with me over 35 years ago.

Excerpts from Letters to Lois Meessen that mention Gören

(November 30, 1967) "…Something else kinda wonderful happened here. I picked up a rider. He was visiting Pierre-qui-Vire and asked to ride with me to EnCalcat. That was Thursday, November 22, and he is still with me. He is Swedish, 20, baptized in spring. He is a happy combination of some of the ideals of hippies, beatniks and Utopians. For me, he has been a most sympathetic companion and has charged my days with more joy than I could ever have in solitary travels."

"We visited Taize (the Protestant monastery). What a pleasure for me to join their prayers. Then EnCalcat. Then Lourdes, but on the way to Lourdes we had car troubles—the first in over 6,000 miles. The vicissitudes of this will have to wait till later, but because of this we were two nights on the road (in small hotels). Then we ran short of French money. I had to use all he had to pay for repairs [to the car]. Most interesting! We were down to about $2 worth of French francs between us. We could not change dollars, travelers' checks or Deutsche Marks into French francs. [For some political reason, France was not accepting any foreign money.] These were moments of some concern for me, believe me. What do you do in a foreign country with a car, no acceptable money for gas, for lodging or for travel to another country? We had only about 24 hours with this concern, but it was real. We shared a room one night, and a bed the next and we have survived with a sense of humor. He is like something out of Irish mythology for me, though he might not be allowed in Greece for his disheveled appearance."

"We are now in a very, very interesting monastery, part of the ruins of which make up what are called "The Cloisters" of the New York Metropolitan

Museum. The way of life here is very special—experimental so to speak. The discipline is less rigid. The fraternity most real. There are only about eight men here and we have been accepted into all their programs."

"I am writing this in the late afternoon after Gören (pronounced Yer-an) and I have had a fantastic trip into the mountains. Besides climbing around the top of the mountains we stopped twice—once at my suggestion—that we go down to the shore of a rushing stream to listen to the sounds of tumbling, gushing water—the other at his—that we drink from a stream cascading down a precipice. What fun we have with the simplicity of children as we enjoy the wonders of nature and man around us."

(December 2, 1967. Saint Michel de Cuxa) "Leaving today for Montserrat. Have had a wonderful experience here. The life is very, very simple. Also Gören and I have romped the mountains and valleys with delight. He speaks English well and is able to enjoy the little niceties of language that make conversation fun. (He speaks about six languages.)"

(December 19, 1967 at Beuron, Germany) "As I write this in mid-afternoon, a few feet away on a sofa sleeps the little pixy. Gören did not stay in Spain as he had planned, but accompanied me to Rome. After parting there, he later came to a decision to return home for Christmas and has been with me ever since. He has long since lost any great interest in the monasteries we visit, but he is good company traveling and puts up with me. He is very sensitive to beauty, and we have been flooded with it in the thousands of miles we have traveled in France, Spain, Italy, Austria, Switzerland and Germany. He heads for Sweden Friday—exactly a month since we left Pierre-qui-Vire together."

Addenda

This is not meant to be a biography, but I would like to capture a few more moments from this fleeting encounter.

I had a Leica camera with me and I took a picture of Gören and me and our car in the Pyrenees Mountains. The Leica had a special feature of delayed shots, so I was able to get into the picture.

We were both on a tight budget. We did little eating out. What we usually did was to purchase the makings of sandwiches and then eat along the way. Our main meal was usually in monasteries.

I remember with particular joy the day we first saw the Mediterranean Sea. We parked on the highway and went down to the shore with our lunch. Gören was eager to touch the water, so he went to the edge of the water just as a wave of considerable size came crashing in. He got soaked. Since we were in an area not visible from the highway, he took off his pants, wrung them out, and placed them on a huge rock to dry in the sun. We proceeded to break out our baguettes, ham cheese and yogurt and ate our lunch while his pants dried out, well at least got drier than they were. By the way, I also wanted to touch the water, but I did it more carefully after seeing what had happened to him. I took a picture here too but only of him. He was standing on a huge rock and I timed it so that it showed the splash and spray of a high wave striking it. I don't have that picture but I do have one that he took of me in a similar stance, though without much spray.

I could go on and on, but suffice it to say that Gören was an event in my life that I appreciated even at the time, and I have treasured up in my heart ever since.

Yugoslavian Simeon

Balloons and clowns have nothing to do with the religion I was brought up in, and I am still not comfortable with loose expressions about God that move very far from the center of theological discourse. That's part of my baggage. I can live with what that means for me, given my age and the context of my life. Yet I mark, almost to the hour, a liberty of spirit that caught me by surprise and changed my life dramatically, as little else has. The memory of this experience and how it continues to influence my thinking makes me more tolerant of people who fly balloons and speak of Christ as a clown.

A clown is what came to mind that day of which I speak. The thought was not flattering. The train on which I was to spend the night pushing across Europe was already crowded. Not crowded like a New York subway shuttle in rush hour, but crowded in the peculiar way European thru-trains can be in the summer months. Baggage and people had already spilled out of the compartments and into the aisles. Here was this character, right out of Dickens, on a fantastic high, popping in and out of our compartment to hang out the window, to holler hellos to any and all standing on the platforms of the depots. He was loud. I mean really loud. As he reached out the window to wave, his sweater would pull up and his sweatpants pull down till much of his backside was left exposed.

Yet this young man made a profound impression on me. I record the incident because it is one of the few occasions in my life for which I have a record. Not infrequently, we express the importance of a given moment in our lives. Only time can tell. Now, some 14 years later, I can from a better perspective say again that the young Yugoslavian became and continues to be a Christ-figure for me. Here is how I recorded the incident in a journal entry dated early July 1967:

> *I was still inexperienced in Eurail travel and so at Ostend, seeing the train was crowded, I took the first seat I could find. It was in 2nd class. (With my pass I was entitled to travel in 1st class. Believe me, that is a big difference.) And this train went all the way to Yugoslavia. That was bad news. Everybody seemed to have decided to go there this night. I had heard of people standing for two days and nights in trains. I now see how it would be possible. The aisles were stacked with baggage and people.*

Strangely enough, it was this night that I had a most moving experience. At Brussels, the whole Yugoslavian quarter must have been down to meet the train. Some to come on—others to see them off. There was one open seat in our compartment. Four big men came in. They were an escort for a little old lady. Come to find out the other 18 were outside the window cheering her on. The general noise level was that of a Notre Dame alumni party—third down and some to go. The general idea was that they wished her well, liked her a lot, etc. She must have been in her seventies or eighties and spoke Yugoslavian well, but that wouldn't be much good in Belgium and Germany. She was a nimble creature, and before the night was far spent, had assumed every position humanly possible without being on her head. She had a window seat, and at one point, she had turned completely around with her feet up in front of her on the seat and her back against the little platform that serves as a table for the window seats.

Above all the din of these farewells was the voice of a young man somewhere between 16 and 24. He was in purple sweat pants and a bright red sweatshirt. When he leaned out the window to shout to friends—which he frequently did—these two articles of clothing became strangers to each other, exposing to the fresh air large areas of vertebrae. He was everywhere. Waving, shouting, whistling, hanging out the window, he became rather conspicuous. But I noted him most because he took it upon himself to watch over Grandma. Whenever a ticket agent or a customs official came near the compartment, he had to deal with this gallant protector. Grandma never had to say a word. The young man would pop in, take her papers and ticket and, in general protect her. As I watched this young uninhibited gentleman perform, I had a growing impression of being in the presence of a Christ-figure. For a while, he had no seat. He worked out from a suitcase in the corridor. Whenever a new passenger appeared at the head of the aisle he would dash out to help carry suitcases. He was in the general area of our compartment to watch over Grandma. If someone took out a cigarette, he would pop in with a match to light it. Whenever he took out his cigarettes, he offered them all around. It was a master performance of uninhibited generosity.

When eventually a seat became available, he joined us and I learned a little about him. When he learned I was an American, he was ecstatic. He told me the real loves of his life were Elvis Presley and the "Stones." He had seen all the Presley films many times. I might have hoped for more, but it in no way lessened my admiration for him. This night with him did more to unshackle my self-conscious inhibitions in dealing with others than any other one factor. I thought of him frequently all summer long and, because of his example, I felt freer to try to be "Christ to others" as I rode the rails and moved about in railroad stations. I will never forget that train ride and I will always be grateful for the good example I was given by a young man who, by some standards, might be a reject from society. May God bless him.

On July 29, 1967, that same summer, I wrote to a friend:

> *You would have been proud of me Monday. I was like a young man in love—like my little Yugoslavian friend who was going home. I helped two ladies with language problems, paid in Marks for people short of change, offered to pay to let two nuns, who were standing, into 1st class. I sat them in our compartment and then cornered the conductor in the corridor. He let them stay there. I jumped up and opened doors and carried suitcases for people too loaded down.*
>
> *In the railway station at Innsbruck, I saw a couple (elderly) resting halfway up the steps. I dropped my bags and went over and carried theirs for them. It was such fun!*

I can honestly say that the rest of that summer I was like a different person. I consciously tried to make myself a silent Christ-figure. The experience was exhilarating.

Inhibitions have come back, and I am not as free a person as I was that summer. Down deep inside me, though, is the Jugoslavian Simeon, eager to be an *alter Christus*.

The idea was not new to me in 1967, but it became more a part of me then, surprised by a clown in a passing moment on a crowded train.

Report on a Sabbatical Leave in 1967

In 1967, sabbaticals were talked about, but were not a part of the academic experience. I asked for one. I was refused by the College, but approved by the School of Theology. It was a delicate impasse. However, having jumped through many hoops, I was allowed to go. This is a report when I returned. The piece reflects my being a little apologetic for not producing a research paper as a product of my time off. Reading this now, almost 40 years later, I am touched by the report. That period truly was a defining moment in my life. Many of the little stories, included above, date from that period: Ode to a Mosquito, An Afternoon in Düssledorf, A Reflection on a Storm at Sea, Jugoslavian Simeon, and Göran Ogen. There could be as many more. The original document included lists of libraries visited and a progress report on titles purchased. I omit them here.

During the nine months from May 1967 to January 1968, I was privileged to visit Europe. My passage was paid for by a friend; my travels supported by work. Besides the opportunity to encounter other cultures, I had some specific goals in mind. Traveling as a librarian, I wanted to visit what libraries I could; to learn more of cooperative programs among Catholic theological libraries; to search for books. In the process, I hoped to broaden my own horizons as much as I could.

That I was able to do something toward each of these goals, there is no doubt in my mind. I am not unaware of how much I was not able to do for one reason or another. The program I set up to support the trip considerably conditioned the extent and mode of travel.

From June 14 to November 1, I worked as a civilian chaplain with the American Military Services in Europe. I regularly offered Mass on Saturday, heard confessions on Saturday and Sunday, and had a morning and evening Mass on Sunday. These services were all at Heidelberg, Germany. My movements in this period were all conditioned on my need to be in Heidelberg on the weekend, leaving me free to move about Monday through Friday.

Advantages derived from this program:

- Apostolic work kept alive religious ideals and obligations.

- A home base was provided to work from and return to—an important physical and psychological pulse for me as time went on.

- The funds accrued from the military supported my movements about Europe.

As disadvantages of this weekend work, I would say:

- It kept me from extending travel, of continuing a journey, and thus considerably cut down on opportunities to get to some places at all, or to remain in others of interest for a time.

- It kept me closely dependent on the American community so that my contacts with Europeans in depth were minimal.

These are facts I lived with. I would like now to give some indication of how I feel the above goals were filled.

Attached to this report a list of the libraries I visited will be found. In some of them, I made only a casual visit, while I spent many hours in the others. As a visiting librarian, I was afforded special consideration and had guided tours by staff members in most of these libraries. With special pleasure, I recall the personal treatment I received at such major institutions as:

> Bibliotheque National, Paris; Bibliotheque Royale, Brussels; Stadt Bibliothek, Vienna; Stadt Bibliothek, Trier; The Royal Library, Copenhagen; and Vatican Library, Rome.

On October 14, in Frankfort, I was an official observer at a meeting of the Cooperative Council for the Theological Library Associations of Europe. Present were the heads of the national theological library organizations of Belgium, Netherlands, France, Germany and Italy. A representative of the Catholic Library Association of America flew over to be present for this meeting. Counting lunch, it was a six-hour meeting. The programs and policies that they are striving for have been, for the most part, already achieved in the states: Standards for libraries, trained librarians, budget, union list of serials, etc.

As a result of this meeting, an attempt was made to interest the Congregation of Universities and Seminaries to establish minimal standards for seminary libraries. The attempt was unsuccessful, as I have come to understand. In any case, our library more than meets the standards they were recommending.

There was a strong sense of mission among these men to accomplish what they all recognize as an uphill task. Although there are notable exceptions, the theological libraries that I saw and that I heard about left much to be desired. They have little money for books and periodicals; they are haphazardly staffed, and their catalogs are only as accurate and consistent as the men who have the job. They lack the aids and tools, such as classification systems or subject heading guides or the Library of Congress, such as we enjoy.

My quest for books was not as easy as I had supposed. The kind of shopping I have come to enjoy in many secondhand bookstores in the States was not encouraged. Most bookstores displayed very little stock and the dealers preferred to search for specific titles. Although I had a list of *desiderata*, it consisted mostly of items very hard to locate. Attached is a brief report submitted to the Dean of Theology regarding use I made of a gift. I did have one week at Oxford in Blackwell's and Thornton's that was particularly rewarding.

I am very much aware that I have become an authority on nothing in these months. I have many, many impressions and have made some personal judgments, but in all of what follows I offer the reflections of an observer. In my own mind, the broadening aspect of this trip was most rewarding.

As a librarian, I learned:

- that the European system is less patron-oriented than American libraries.
- that classification systems differ from place to place.
- that theology libraries may be rich in collections of ancient tomes, but inadequately kept up to date.
- that vast collections of rare and precious volumes are fascinating and thrilling to see and use, but they are only a small aspect of the service a library should provide.

As an American citizen, I was made to reflect on such things as:

- our lack of border formalities between states.
- the single official language of the States.
- the divisive character of language and culture.
- advantages and disadvantages of a long history and old buildings.
- our single monetary system.

- trains that run on time; bicycles and motor scooters; high cost of gas.

- the unpopularity of Americans in many places of Europe; tourism, pros and cons.

As a Catholic, I was:

- impressed by the cathedrals and churches, but skeptical of the effectiveness of the Church in society.

- charmed by the villages visibly dominated by their churches.

- disturbed by the mammoth churches in areas of great poverty; by the lack of vocations.

- disappointed with liturgical celebrations.

As a monk, I was:

- warmed by the spirit of charity that welcomed me as a brother into community after community.

- pleased to be able to concelebrate in eight different countries.

- privileged to visit 32 different monasteries and follow the *horarium* in most of them.

How does one measure the other values he derives from such a tour? What do "moments" do to one's life and spirit? I have no answer to that, but I know I was personally enriched beyond my greatest expectations. I recall as "moments" such things as:

- absorbing the silent beauty of sunsets over Iceland, Rhodes, Copenhagen and Rome.

- standing at the Berlin Wall and being shaken to the roots with the horror of what it stands for.

- listening with tears to the JFK speech at the Schönberg Rathaus, *Ich bin ein Berliner.*

- drinking water from a cascading brook in the Pyrenees and free beer at the Carlsburg Brewery in Copenhagen.

- crawling over the Grecian ruins in Athens, Delphi, Corinth and Cape Sounion.

- racing madly down the *Autobahn* and winding through the tortuous alleys of medieval towns.

- following the windings of the picturesque Danube and the busy Rhine.

- swimming in the Mediterranean and Baltic seas and talking shop with seminarians over wine in Innsbruck.

- creeping down the jet-black corridors of Mont César at night and fighting traffic in the bright white light of an Athenian sun.

- standing at the graveside of Fr. Guy Ferrari, my classmate, buried in Rome, in a downpour.

- praying alone at a wayside shrine, and joining with 40 Benedictines from all over Europe as they chanted office in the Anglican Cathedral of Coventry.

These and many more, like the hour at St. Mary, Virgin, in Oxford, are moments I have treasured.

More than events and sights in themselves, I felt shaped by the people I met. In time, I came to count these contacts more influential than all the building I saw or places I visited. I experienced a blossoming of my own personality I would be hard put to define, but which was nonetheless very real to me:

- the Jugoslavian who was a Christ-figure in a crowded train.

- Göran, the young Swede, who loved beauty and who shared my fortunes for a month.

- David, the Lutheran minister, and Carol, his wife; they took me in.

But why go on? I could fill a page with such names as Fr. Hildebrand, Anselm and Romuald; Lois and Teddy and Eric; Dave and Joyce, Gordon and Wanda; Joe, Len and Claude.

If some of this enthusiasm seems naïve in a man 45 and counting, perhaps it is not out of place to note that this was the first such experience of my life. Anyway, it is a part of me now. Whatever direction my life and work may take in the future, I feel I will always be indebted to this time of grace.

On Doing Damage

"I want to do damage!" My friend frequently speaks these sentiments in various ways that include the word "damage." "I am looking forward to doing damage." "I want to be engaged where I can do the most damage."

I do not know the English word for the opposite of euphemism. A euphemism is a word that expresses a thought less offensively. "Damage" is a bad way of saying something good. It is like the street talk that says, "He's bad" and means "He's good."

It was a little jarring to me at first, but I've come to like the expression, and I find myself when heading for church, and on other occasions, saying to myself, "I'm going to do some damage."

Institutions and entities that depend on benefaction to do their work reach out to their friends and ask for some share of the time, talent and treasure. Some can respond with all three, some with two and some with one. For the most part, these benefactors buy into the mission they support and are happy to be of some help. In the parlance of this essay, they are doing damage.

Those not so blessed with financial resources can be richly supportive by sharing of their time and talent by serving on boards, by participation in committee work, by contacting people of means who share the values that the institution fosters. These are all ways of doing damage.

Another way anyone can contribute to a cause is by prayer. They can ask God to prosper the work being done. They can pray to God to provide guidance, wisdom and means to accomplish the ideal goals that have been laid out. Prayer is an added dimension to the opportunities to further the ideals of a religious institution.

The gentleman referred to above uses all these means and I have come to appreciate deeply what he intends when he says he wants to make a difference. He just says it differently. Now I, with him, want to focus more on doing damage.

A Difficult Moment, 1946

In the fall of 1946, the Saint Meinrad Abbey Chapter voted to promote Marmion Priory to the rank of Abbey. The personnel of the founding community were pretty much in place. Some of the monks had already given years to the work there and wanted to continue. However, a certain number of monks would be assigned to the fledgling community from the ranks of the Abbey. As is customary, each one had the opportunity to submit a preference: 1) join the new community; 2) be willing to go if chosen; and 3) prefer to remain a member of the Saint Meinrad community. It was understood, of course, that we might not get our preference, but that the superiors would make every effort to honor it, especially no. 3.

I can say categorically that I did not want to change my vow of stability to Marmion. However, in a spirit of detachment, I opted for 2, i.e., I would be willing to go if sent. That left me somewhat on pins and needles for the brief period when the founding members were being designated. Because Fr. Columban Reed recruited me while he was trying to get students to come to Marmion, it was only reasonable that they might make a claim on me. Whether they did or not, I do not know, but my perception was that they did. And that left me uneasy.

One Sunday morning before the Conventual Mass, I got a message that Fr. Abbot wanted to see me right after Mass. It would be hard to describe the turmoil I experienced for the next hour or so. I made profound acts of resignation as I struggled, distracted, all through the liturgy. Finally, the Mass was over and I was on the threshold of Fr. Abbot's office.

I entered and knelt to kiss his ring, as was the custom of the time. After I rose, he pointed to an article in a Catholic paper, lying on his desk, about a young monk at Benet Lake who was an alumnus of our schools. Fr. Abbot remarked on the success of people who go elsewhere after they had been here for a while. My heart sank even further.

Fr. Abbot then rather apologetically asked me to cut his hair. It was Sunday. The request was rather unusual for a holy day. I was ecstatic. Being a barber was not one of my favorite assignments, but I never, before or after, performed my trade with more joy and utter relief than I did that haircut on a Sunday morning. I had dodged the draft!

An Essay on Spirituality of Saint Meinrad

Readers may find this a bit much to digest. It was a project of my last sabbatical and was written for possible inclusion in a book of essays commemorating our 150th jubilee. By the time I had finished it, I recognized that it had become more of a personal recollection than an objective study and I did not have the energy to make it right. I felt better about the piece after I had found an article by Fr. Jean LeClercq, O.S.B., on early monasticism that listed something like 17 different themes/values of early monasticism. I was able to find most of them couched within the text one way or another. I include this essay here because it might just shed some insight on living the life of a monk in my time.

How does one measure the spirituality of a community? The challenge is to try to get as accurate a pulse as one can realizing that in the end there is no measuring rod, or thermometer, available to us that can accomplish the task. The approach of this essay is to examine such written documents as we may have that might throw light on the subject and then rely on anecdotal reports to fill in the picture.

The centrality of the Divine Office and the Sacred Liturgy to the life of this community is patent and is reported elsewhere. The private prayer life or the devotional life of the members is not reported till now.

There were two novitiates in the community, one for fraters (brothers enrolled in the School of Theology, destined for a clerical role in the Church) and the one for lay brothers. The lay brothers did not participate in the full round of liturgical prayers, but the presumption here is that they had a formation in prayer and devotion that was mostly the same as the Fraters'. Certainly, they participated in all the novenas, Marian devotions, June devotions, etc. with the rest of the community. There were probably times when parallel devotions were conducted in German for them, at least in the early days. In particular, the brothers recited the rosary in German.

Father Abbot Ignatius Esser started a new program to initiate Americans into the community of brothers. He began receiving "oblates" into the Oblate School, called St. Placid Hall. It was a high school for young men who wanted to be Brothers in the community. It had a regular academic program and a formation program, but it also included learning a trade. Considerable planning went into the project of introducing the young men into the monastery. A separate administration for the "junior brothers" went into effect as the first graduates from St. Placid Hall came up to the monastery in the late 1930s. They lived in a separate space; they had their own chapel. A decision was made that they would not just recite the "Little Office of the Blessed Virgin," as was the custom for the German-speaking brothers. A book of hours, called Divine Praise, was created first in mimeographed copies, later in book form, printed at the Abbey Press. I bring it up here because this was a dramatic shift in the prayer life of the brothers. The senior brothers continued to have their separate German round of prayer until the early 1960s when the English office of the junior brothers began to be the only one officially recited in public.

For many of the early years, each novice was handed a *Holy Rule*, a *Novice Manual*, the *Imitatio Christi*, and a small work known as the *Tyrocinium*. Further, it was the custom that each novice wrote out in long hand a set of novice rules that became more elaborate as the years past.

The *Holy Rule* is itself a document of formation. Benedict has disclaimers, but centuries of vital communities of prayer and work give evidence that, with the guidance of a master, it is a tool to shape lives and create a community ethos of reverence for God and concern for one another. The school of the Lord's service is made up of people committed to seeking God, not just in the hours of prayer, but throughout the day and night; not just concerned with rooting out inappropriate behavior, but striving hour by hour and day by day to build up a community of believers permeated with love for one another. Benedict created an *horarium* and a community framework to help that formation take place. His chapters on obedience, on humility, on prayer and on service challenge the interior motivations and attitudes of his monks. There is ample evidence that the novice masters throughout the history of the order have striven to instill the principles of the Rule, and that monks have taken seriously their efforts to be faithful to the ideals laid down. Certainly, Saint Meinrad was not an exception to this long tradition.

In what follows, I will try to list elements of community formation that influenced the quality of the spiritual life of the monks.

Monastic Enclosure. The monastic enclosure is the place where the school of the Lord's service takes place. The quality of that space and the discipline that pervades it creates an atmosphere conducive to monastic living and the discipline and prayer that take place there. While one would not label the *horarium* and the silence in the monastery as devotional, they are the matrix out of which the discipline and devotions flow.

Monastic Decorum. When we were clothed with the habit, we were instructed on some of the dos and don'ts for monks. We were issued two habits, one for work and everyday use, the other for major feast days, i.e., OA's (*Officia Abbatis*). Some were issued a third habit to be used for outside and dirty work. These were little more than rags. Prayers were recited while donning the habit. Habits were to be worn in the house at all times. At the discretion of the superior, habits may or may not be worn for work outside, or for recreation. Not infrequently, we wore the habit at work and at play, including handball and touch football. We took hikes all around the countryside in habits. One did not sit on one's scapular. It was to be pulled aside before sitting. The scapular was not to be thrown over one's shoulder but folded around and tucked into the cincture, a regulation honored more in the breech because of convenience. When walking one does not swing his arms. Whenever not otherwise engaged, the hands were to be kept under the scapular whether walking or sitting. "The habit does not make the monk." However, it, too, was a discipline of formation as one grew into a demeanor that helped preserve serenity, and a consciousness of vocation.

Obedience. I do not intend here to review all the monastic virtues, but obedience, stressed so strongly in the Rule, was reinforced in many small ways. Permission had to be gotten for almost anything outside the normal scheduled activities: to have visitors; to speak to a seminarian; to read a book; at times, even to go to the library; to write home more than once a month; to stay up beyond the hour for going to bed; to see the doctor; to take a nap during a recreation period; and the like. Even recreation was highly regulated. Permission had to be gotten even to sit down when the group was walking. In general, one did only what the group did. The norm in general was: "Follow the example of your senior." No innovations without permission." Seniority was strictly followed in everything. It was always proper to defer to one's senior. These norms were sometimes oppressive, sometimes ridiculous, but always formational. I was corrected once in choir by a senior frater for the way I stood or knelt, I do not remember which. He said I should do only what my seniors did. Not yet as docile as I should have been, for a couple of days I scratched my head, blew my nose, and I do not remember what all, just as he did. As I continued my little ways, I gradually began to realize how ridiculous I was being. I stopped doing those things and accepted the lesson I seemed to have rejected. That I remember that incident over 50 years ago is indication of how it impressed me. In the end, I learned a valuable spiritual principle.

Poverty. The vow of poverty was taken very seriously. St. Benedict remarks that one has given up the rights even to his own body. All possessions were considered as belonging to the community. We were instructed to avoid using "my" in any context. "Our" was to be used instead. Things in daily use were spoken of as "*ad usum,*" i.e. for the use of. Even Fr. Henry's copy of the *Novice Manual,* and mine, have "ad usum," or a.u. for short, on the flyleaf. The vestry was the source of all our clothing and toiletry supplies. Permission was needed to use the items selected. Poverty is still taken very seriously, but today those little niceties of language are out of vogue. Permission is granted for things provided by the vestry without asking. Special purchases can only be made with permission. Benedictine poverty has a quality all its own. Living according to its norms was, and is, a very important factor in the spiritual values of the individual monks and the community as a whole.

Horarium. The *horarium* over the past 150 years has undergone a number of transformations. For around 100 of those years, though, there was little variation in the schedule. Matins and Lauds were at 4 a.m. The other hours of the Divine Office followed. The early hour for prayer preserved a long, monastic tradition of rising in the night to pray. Except for the last three days of Holy Week, when the first service was at 6 a.m., 4 a.m. was the norm, summer and winter, ferial or feast. Not much emphasis was given to this early rising. It amounted to a strong statement of the priority of prayer in the life of the community. The discipline of early rising for prayer implied a willingness to sacrifice the body in order to offer praise and thanksgiving. I once heard Fr. Abbot Ignatius say: "You never get used to getting up early. You just get used to being tired!" It is of interest to note that that *horarium* was set before electricity became a given in the house. The rhythm of early rising and early retiring was more in tune with light and darkness. Even after electrical lights had been installed, for many years, the electricity was shut off between 9 p.m. and 4 a.m. As work and study became more feasible in the evening hours, some mitigation was established for the hour of rising, though in all the various schedules, Morning Prayer has never started later that 5:30 am. I believe that this early morning schedule of reserving the first three to four hours for prayer and meditation is a strong non-verbal statement of devotion. It sets a tone for the interior life of the monks.

Silence. St. Benedict devotes a chapter to the importance of silence. Silence not only disciplines the tongue, but it creates a kind of open space where prayer and recollection can be fostered. After the manner of St. Benedict's fifth chapter, the community has distinguished night silence and day silence. The night silence has always been strictly followed. *Culpa* was called for if silence was broken, and an added penance of five Our Fathers and five Hail Marys was automatically added to whatever penances the superior might impose. Day silence, as it is called, is less strict but always implied. Speaking in the corridors was always considered a breach. Should one need to speak or converse, special spaces were provided. I believe that this discipline has been well observed both in the old monastery and in the new. I have little doubt that the community followed this same pattern in the early years, as I have seen it observed over the past 57. I remember one time in the early '60s. Fr. Barnabas Harrington, who was a very observant monk, returned home after a long session in St. Louis, where he was an apprentice architect. He was a dear friend of mine, and I had been his confessor. It so happened we came out of church together. Our eyes met as such friends' would. We walked the corridor to the refectory in silence, not in any weird feeling of oppression, but respecting each other's wish to observe the discipline of the house. We spoke of it later with mutual appreciation. That is rather personal incident, but I offer it as reflecting the discipline we had been taught and embraced. Occasionally a visitor, unattuned to the discipline, will make the silence almost palpable in its breech. It is presumed that day silence also applied to one's place of work. I am not so confident that day silence was as well observed in the workplace. My work was in the library, where quiet is time-honored. However, I am not conscious that day silence inhibited my speaking there. I have my doubts that silence was observed at the place of work if the work occurred outside the cloister.

Trappist monasteries are known to have developed an elaborate sign language. That was not the case at Saint Meinrad. It is surprising how much can be communicated without talking. Eyes, facial expressions, shoulders, hands were all used to communicate. At table, there were signs for condiments and bread. The one for mustard was rocking the hands like a cradle for a baby. I will not say why mustard was called baby. Even this form of communication is traceable to the *Holy Rule*, where St. Benedict is adamant about silence at table.

Culpa. *Culpa* is the Latin word for fault. Used by monks, it refers to a ritual, both public and private, of admitting to a breech of some sort. It is public when in formal session the community has an opportunity by means of formulas to ask pardon for faults committed. Private *culpa* is a ritual performed by an individual monk admitting to a local superior some breech of discipline. It is not sacramental confession, but it is motivated by some of the same dispositions of spirit. For the most part, *culpa* pertains to the external forum, breeches of community discipline, or spirit, or the like. Some religious communities have sessions for accusing one another of faults for the betterment of the community living. Our *culpa* is not like that. It is self-accusatory. In so far as there is an admission of guilt, it is recognition of human frailty; it curbs pride; it restores the order that has been broken. The superior to whom one recites *culpa* gives some form of penance. For the most part, there are standard formulas for most offenses. Such as: *de effuso fluido* [for spilling water], de schisso vestimento [for tearing my clothes], *de strepitu in dormitorio* [for disturbance in the dormitory (where strict quiet prevailed), *de fracto silencio* for breaking silence], etc. I remember two stories in my time of rather unusual faults. One was "I threw a horse." Another was "I broke a crowbar." For that one, the superior is reported to have shouted, "You WHAT??" I do not know what kind of a penance Frater Julius got. Probably an "*in medio,*" which stood for "*in medio refectorii.*" "*In medio*" meant that one knelt out in the dining room during meal prayers before the meal with a ritual of kissing the floor before proceeding to one's place at table. "*In medio*" went into desuetude during the 1960s and 70s, but has come back in recent years. Of course, all such rituals are conducted in the vernacular now.

A similar practice is kneeling out in church after an office or Mass. This is left to the judgment of the individual. One "kneels out" if he has done something to disturb the choir: dropping a seat, dropping a kneeler or book, failing to intone, or making some egregious mistake in singing or reciting. This practice is *au courant*. In a similar way, one bowed to the altar for more minor infractions. This practice has discontinued.

Formal *culpa* for over a hundred years was a weekly exercise built into the schedule; now it is more seasonal. Private *culpa,* for some years, faded out, but it is one of those monastic practices that have come back. I include a discussion of *culpa* here, not because it is a devotion, but because it is an ascetical practice that nurtures sensitivity to the ways personal negligence offends against charity and discipline so essential to the full living of the monastic life. As the saying goes, "a little humiliation is good for the soul." There is lots of precedence in the *Holy Rule* for this ongoing practice.

Devotional Confession. Along these same lines, devotional confession was encouraged. This was almost a community exercise. After supper on Friday evenings, priest-confessors would be in their cells. Monks lined up outside the cell of the confessor of their choice. This was an ascetical and sacramental practice much recommended by spiritual directors. Exactly when this practice was introduced, if it wasn't from the beginning, I do not know. I presume that it came from Einsiedeln. Some religious communities encouraged almost daily, devotional confession. That was not the case at Saint Meinrad. Actually, very little was said about it officially, but the exercise was a given. In these latter years, probably from the late 1960s, the emphasis has been on having a spiritual director and/or a confessor. The rest is left to the individual. The Friday night silence for confession has been dropped.

Fast and Abstinence. Fasting during Lent was Church law and was observed scrupulously by those between the ages of 21 and 60. As a special kind of penance, breakfast, consisting of bread, butter, jelly or honey, and coffee, was taken kneeling down. Meat was served once a day, but not on Wednesdays and Fridays, as Church law decreed for days of abstinence. Those not fasting were served the same fare. By and large, we were served a meat-and-potatoes diet with a heavy hand. Pie and cake were not uncommon, but other delicacies were. Not a few monks found the regimen difficult. I remember Fr. Dunstan, a rather hefty man, warning a class, in a morning hour at the beginning of Lent, not to unduly try his patience because the diet left him in a foul mood.

Monastic fast and abstinence was of a different order. It was a more mitigated restriction at meals. In a designated period from September to Easter, Monday, Wednesday and Friday were days of monastic fast. No eating between meals was permitted. On non-fast days, one might have fruit, or some other candy or food, during afternoon recreation period only. The bell for the end of recreation was the official signal closing down all eating outside meals. There was an expression "1:30 fruit stops," which indicated the end of the open period for food. It was said, perhaps only in jest, that Fr. Stephen Thuis, novice master for only a brief period, got a migraine headache when one of the fraters admitted he had eaten fruit after 1:30.

Preoccupation with food, any excessive hankering for delicacies and the like, has been the target of ascetics from the earliest time. Eating and drinking easily lead to excess. Most spiritual regimens find food and drink a frontline battleground. Perhaps because these functions are so measurable, beginning programs start there. Some might say that the monastic fare in those days was mortification enough. That is certainly not true today in most houses and at Saint Meinrad in particular. Fasting is time-honored in the Church and in monastic tradition. It was not otherwise at Saint Meinrad, though in my time I do not remember much official emphasis being placed on its exercise. It was expected of a monk and that was that.

There has been some shift in worldviews in monastic communities. Spaces are set aside for some repast outside the meal and recreation periods. Coffeebreaks have been introduced. The point here being that fraternal camaraderie and good communication can take place in these informal settings, and that could be seen as a greater good than mortification. Monks whose worldview did not shift saw such shenanigans as scandalous. I remember back in a period before this more-mitigated position had been taken, a sign posted on a coffee urn by Fr. Abbot Ignatius. It said: "If you are sick, go to bed. The infirmarian will take care of you. There is no excuse for healthy monks eating and drinking outside the regular hours." One can understand how a conscientious religious might struggle with the present practice if he did not know or buy into the theory of its usefulness.

Holy Water. This may seem like a rather strange heading, but for much of our monastic history the use of holy water was as much a part of our day as the air we breathed. Again, I am not prepared to say when the practice of blessing oneself over and over throughout the day was introduced. What I can say is that the practice was firmly entrenched by the time I came to the monastery in 1943, and I would be prepared to suggest that the practice had been around for a long, long time before, probably even from Einsiedeln. The practice of signing oneself with holy water combined two rituals deeply established in the history of the Christian life. Every room in the house had a holy water font. One of the regular, weekly duties of the novices was to fill up a spouted water-can at the container of holy water in the St. John the Baptist Chapel of the Abbey Church and make the rounds of every room. The routine was to knock first, open the door only enough to perform your little duty, say "Holy Water," then close the door and move on.

I would not claim this to be an exclusive monastic practice. In fact, this was another practice about which little or nothing was said. It was the Christian custom of the time. Many of us had holy water fonts in the rooms of our homes. Meant to keep us in touch with our Baptism and its promises, it also was an instrument in repelling the wiles of the devil. Of course, the sign of the cross over one's body was already an established practice in the second century. It is not an exaggeration to say that one might cross himself three to five times in the course of a minute as he moved from room to room. The very excessive use in the past may have reduced its meaningfulness. The practice has not been dropped. Now it is used primarily on entering church, as a reminder of our Baptism and as a kind of purification rite before entering the sacred space.

I might note that the transition was not always easy for all. In times we sometimes call turbulent, some wanted to drop the practice completely. Until that time, a frater was assigned to stand by the holy water font to dispense the holy water to the monks passing by in ranks in the center of the corridor. Sometimes the frater would not appear. Then the monk on the left, as the community entered the church in pairs, would have to step out of ranks to reach the font, wet his fingers, and then pass his wetted hand to his partner. Occasionally, the one on the left for personal reasons would not reach for the Holy Water. That meant that the one on the right either also had to do without, or make a political statement by leaving ranks to reach for the holy water himself. I remember this tense little drama going on for several weeks, until some genius put another font on the other side of the corridor so that each could take or not take the holy water as he preferred. Peace at last.

Along that same line, I had a personal lesson on how slow change can come about in the monastery. Before the Chapter Room was renovated in 1942-43, the holy water font was about six feet from the door. It was the responsibility of a novice to stand between the door and the font to facilitate the passing of holy water as monks entered for spiritual reading or for other exercises. In the renovated Chapter Room, the font was located in the doorpost itself. Our class was the first to be received in the renovated room. When it came my turn, as a novice, to distribute Holy Water there, I found it rather ridiculous to be stationed there for the distribution of the water, and I said so to my superior. I was commanded to do what I was told. The practice went on with the novice frequently bumping shoulders with the incoming monks for at least another year. Monasteries do not rush into change, and over the years, I have noticed how we continue to do little things that no longer have a purpose, or better, the purpose for which they were created is no longer practiced.

Visits to Altars and Shrines. In a number of places in this essay, I have spoken of "visits." We are familiar with the use of the word in this way. We speak of making a visit to a church, or of visiting the Blessed Sacrament. Such expressions were and are a part of our Christian culture. I remember as a boy, before churches were locked up like banks, I was taught to make a visit whenever I walked past a Catholic Church, and for the most part I did. A very impressive development of that practice in the monastery was the visits to altars and shrines in the evening after compline. It was quite common for a goodly number of monks to stay back in church in order to visit various altars and shrines. The most popular shrine was Our Lady of Einsiedeln, where it was not uncommon to see ten to 15 monks kneeling for a few moments in private prayer. Other altars visited were St. John the Baptist, St. Benedict, St. Joseph, Our Lady of Lourdes, and St. Benedict in the Crypt. There was a kneeler in front of an image of the Holy Face of Jesus. A few of the older brothers stopped there. Devotion to the Holy Face was very popular around the turn of the century. Now we practically never hear of it. Visiting altars was not something I remember being taught to do. I did it at first because I saw monks I respected very highly do it regularly. Those few moments each evening became very formational for me. The practice died out when the Abbey Church was renovated in 1969. Some monks still visit the Einsiedeln shrine. Quite a number make regular visits to the Blessed Sacrament.

Night Scapular. A little known and now almost forgotten artifact of monastic life at Saint Meinrad was the night scapular. This was a small swath of the same material as our scapular, probably about 12" x 16" with a hole for placing it over your head. This piece was neatly folded on the pillow during the day and worn at night. It was one more little reminder of our commitment that extended through day and night. I feel sure I wore mine for almost ten years. I have no recollection of why or when I stopped wearing it. My suspicion is that it was not issued to young clerics much into the 1950s.

Spiritual Reading. There were two scheduled periods of spiritual reading each day.

Public spiritual reading was a community exercise prior to compline each evening. Fraters were assigned as readers on a weekly basis. I believe the book selection was done by the prior, though I know that Fr. Abbot Ignatius would not hesitate to insert a title for reading. For the most part, the selections were not heavy reading. This exercise obviously was meant to nurture our spiritual life. There are probably lists of the books read somewhere. The reading was done in the Chapter Room. This public reading was also a buffer period after all the activities of the day in preparation for compline and night silence. Every effort was made to have everyone present for the night blessing during and after compline. I remember reading that in the early days, a signal was devised to ring in the kitchen so that any brothers still working there could get to church in time for the night blessing with holy water by the abbot or prior.

A little footnote to that night blessing. If one had to miss compline for any reason, he was expected to get a night blessing, on his knees, right after supper, or go privately to the superior later in the evening for such a blessing.

Another form of public reading is at table. For more than a century, there was reading at both the noon and evening meal. Not all selections would be considered spiritual. The noon reading might be a secular book; the evening reading was of a more religious flavor. I remember monks telling that volumes of Pastor's "Lives of the Popes" were read at supper. Currently, there is no reading at the noon meal, except on Sundays. Selections for the evening meal may be religious or secular, but presumably inspirational. Visitors find this ancient practice, even referred to in the *Rule*, as quaint. We, for the most part, find it enriching. The reading of a portion of the *Holy Rule* every day and reading the martyrology for the next day has continued from the beginning till now.

The other scheduled period of reading was for private spiritual reading. For the fraters, private spiritual reading was done in common. After 4:00 Vespers, all the monks were expected to go either to the study hall or to their cells for spiritual reading on their knees. Each monk's cell was equipped with a prie-dieu of sorts for this exercise and for other periods of private prayer. The fraters had kneelers at their desks. On feast days, one could sit. This was a half-hour exercise. I know that I had occasion to visit several monks' cells during that period and was edified to see that they were observing their spiritual reading on their knees, just as the fraters and junior brothers were. I remember one father complaining about Fr. Dunstan, mentioned above, because he had the bad habit of drumming his fingers on the prie-dieu as he knelt and read.

In a later incarnation of the schedule, a spiritual reading bell was rung at 4:30. Monks were expected to be doing spiritual reading at that time. The exercise was an expectation, was frequently encouraged, but not policed, as St. Benedict recommended. I for one found it almost impossible to keep that schedule because of my work. Our most recent schedule captures two periods of at least a half-hour each a day, one in the morning between breakfast and Mass, and one after Vespers and before supper. I think it is safe to say that spiritual reading is more treasured now than ever. It should be added that the concept of *lectio divina* is deeply ingrained into the ethos of the community. I would not dare to point to the former practice and say it was not *lectio*, but the approach to Scripture and other reading is different today than it was even 30 years ago.

St. Benedict designates Lent as a special time for holy reading. He clearly states that each is to receive a book to read completely and thoroughly. That must have been a challenge to the librarian, whose library would have been nothing like ours today. St. Benedict wrote his *Rule* almost a thousand years before printing was introduced. What they had were manuscripts, mostly the writings of the Fathers and Scripture. At Saint Meinrad, I am sure customs varied about this, though each monk was and is expected to follow the *Rule* in this regard. In the particular period that I was in the fratery, the assistant novice master, Fr. Claude, dispensed all reading. This rule was not just during Lent. Even if one got a book from the library, one had to get permission to read it. As I recall, we did not find the requirement oppressive, but of a piece with the way our lives were regulated. For most of my period in the clericate, I chose readings from the set of Migne's *Patrologia Latina*, which lined our study hall walls. Permission was not required for that.

Spiritual reading, both public and private, continues to be what it has been through the centuries—an important formational exercise for the interior life of the monk.

Bells. I can imagine that it may be difficult for persons outside a closed community to appreciate the important role bells play in the daily life of Saint Meinrad. Bells filter through our day like threads in a pattern. Some may feel it is stretching things a bit to include bells in a discussion of the devotional life of a community. Not me. In times past, I have waxed poetic about the bells. What I wrote 25 years ago is still true today. Little has changed in the patterns of ringing them.

They are rung for fifteen minutes daily for Morning Prayer and evening prayer. They are rung daily for Mass and Noon Prayer. They are tolled at the death of any of the brethren (one toll for each year of profession). The Angelus continues to be rung morning, noon and evening. They are rung on special occasions, such as the death of a president or the election of a pope. They used to be rung at the consecration at the Conventual Mass. There also was a toll at 3 p.m. every Friday in honor of the Passion of our Lord. Monks were expected to kneel and pray no matter where they were or what they were doing. I remember a number of times at St. Placid Lake when monks in swimming gear knelt at 3 p.m. on Friday while the bell tolled.

Our bells are not automatic. A live monk stands under them and pulls the ropes that make them peal. The person assigned to ring them gets a good lesson in faithful responsibility. No one remarks their ringing. Everyone, it seems, notes if one is late in ringing them. In the *Holy Rule*, the responsibility is the abbot's. The bell-ringer is his delegate.

Bona Opera. The *Bona Opera*, traceable to the *Holy Rule*, is a monastic exercise. Before the beginning of Lent, each monk prepares a document pledging himself to some extra prayer or penance for the duration of Lent. These are meant to be over and above the ecclesiastical fast and abstinence and other community penances. The *Bona Opera* is submitted to the abbot for his blessing. Some such added penances might be: no alcoholic beverages, give up desserts, visits to the cemetery, extra visits to the Blessed Sacrament, daily Stations of the Cross, daily rosary, and the like. This practice is still in place, and has branched out into the oblate program so that many oblates also follow this practice. The formula for the *Bona Opera* is very precise. Usually Fr. Abbot will sign the document before it is handed back. He also usually offers some pious note to each person's formula, encouraging perseverance in good works.

Care of the sick and aged. St. Benedict goes out of his way to stress the importance of care of the sick and aged. The charity and care given in this area is a good barometer of a healthy community. I believe that sensitivity in this area has always been high. It certainly has been since I have been in the community. In the most recent 30 years, we have had the services of Brother Daniel Linskens, who has taken quality medical care to a very high level. We have always had to rely on local doctors who have been very dedicated, but the presence of Br. Daniel in the house and the quality of professional care he has been able to provide is remarkable. Happily, Fr. Anselm is in nurse's training to assist and carry on the work Brother Daniel has been doing. The creation of an infirmary wing in the new monastery has also contributed dramatically to the program. For some years now, we have had nurse in five days a week, and nurse's aides 24 hours a day and seven days a week. I am one who has taxed its resources and enjoyed its services.

Devotions. Under this generic head, I would like to reflect on a number of religious exercises that manifest the religious priorities of the community. The public devotions reflect the official position of the community. Some others grow out of basic Catholic doctrines. Some come from a Benedictine tradition. Some may reflect Catholic culture of the period. Private devotions reflect how the spiritual ethos is incorporated into the lives and actions of individual members of the community. In any case, I believe these devotions make a powerful statement about the faith of the Saint Meinrad community.

To Jesus Christ. I have stated elsewhere that community exercises were strongly Christo-centric. Visits to the Blessed Sacrament were expected before and after almost every exercise.

The whole community, after lunch and supper, gathered in the church for a "visit" and for some exercise of prayer.

Benediction was celebrated after Vespers every Sunday.

The "40 Hours" devotion was celebrated annually, during which there was perpetual adoration. (Four monks, at least, were expected to be in the sanctuary at all times.)

Corpus Christi was celebrated with elaborate decorations in the church and all around the grounds. On that day, a solemn procession around the buildings was held with the abbot carrying the Blessed Sacrament. Two or three special altars would be set up along the way, where the blessing with the Sacrament took place. The bells would ring. Hymns were sung. A marching band played.

Benediction was celebrated every day of May, June and October in connection with special devotions during those months. The June devotions were in honor of the Sacred Heart. I remember hearing singing in a cell as I walked down the corridor one evening. It was Br. Philip singing the hymns for benediction. It was quite unusual to hear such sounds in the corridor. Radios were not allowed so it was quite rare that such sounds were heard. I learned from some of the monks in neighboring cells that Br. Philip "had benediction" every evening about 8 o'clock. He sang all the hymns and recited all the prayers. It was a bit odd, but it showed how deeply the devotion had penetrated his personal life.

The *Novice Manual* had prayers: Monthly Devotion of the Confraternity of the Most Holy Sacrament, which started with an Act of Atonement to Jesus in the Most Holy Sacrament.

In July, a novena in honor of the Precious Blood of Jesus was provided (1889 ed.). This was not included in the third edition, and was not in vogue when I entered the monastery.

Stations of the Cross were held once a week during Lent. Many monks put daily Stations of the Cross in their *"Bona Opera."* The Stations were a popular devotion for some all year round. I heard a story from an old priest in another monastery. He said his monastic cell was next door to a small, brothers' chapel. A pious, elderly brother was accustomed to come to the chapel long before Morning Prayer every day to pray the Stations in the dark. One morning he was off by one door and Fr. Thomas bumped into the brother in his cell.

There was a rubric in the liturgy that one bowed his head at the name of Jesus. This practice was extended to any time the name of Jesus was pronounced in public, a practice still honored by many. This was not just a monastic practice, but was part of Catholic culture of the time. Again, this pious practice is still kept up by some of the older monks.

There was a lifesize crucifix at the foot of the stairs on the first floor of the old monastery. It was a constant reminder of our Lord's love for us, and the suffering He endured on our behalf. I am sure it evoked many a pious reflection. I noticed that the feet of the crucifix were well worn. I was told that many of the senior brothers kissed the cross on the way to morning office. I know, in particular, that this was a pious practice of Brother Odilo. After he had retired in old age from his job as shoemaker, he had a regular routine around 11 o'clock every morning. He would start out at the foot of that cross, and then proceed to the crypt where he prayed before St. Benedict's shrine, then at the Shrine of Our Lady of Lourdes. From there he proceeded up to make a visit to the Blessed Sacrament. He would then walk around to the front of the church on the outside, stopping only to light up a pipe and take a little smoke. After that, he would conclude his rounds at the Einsiedeln chapel. I was so edified by him that I wanted my brother to meet him on an occasion of Tom's visiting me. Since I knew Brother's routine, we waited for him a little after 11 on the north side of church. He was right on schedule. There could be many such stories. The older brothers were especially edifying in their devotions. Brother Clement spent several hours a day sitting in front of the St. Joseph altar.

Whenever one entered the cell, office or classroom, the proper expression was *Laudetur Jesus Christus, Gelobt sei Jesus Christus,* or Praised be Jesus Christ. The response was *In aeternum, In alle Ewigkeit,* or Now and forever. Again, this custom is still practiced by some the older monks.

To Mary. Devotion to Mary is quite notable at Saint Meinrad. This is well within the Benedictine tradition. Although St. Benedict makes no mention of Mary in the *Holy Rule*, devotion to the Blessed Virgin has been an integral part of the tradition, and Saint Meinrad is no exception. After all, it was founded from a monastery in Switzerland that had a long history of being a place of Marian pilgrimage. Our Lady of Einsiedeln is the patroness of the Abbey Church. In the early days of that church, there was a small chapel, within the church, dedicated to her with her image above the altar. A shrine in her honor has always been a part of the church. Processions to the shrine, with singing of the various seasonal Marian antiphons, were always a weekly tradition, until the mid-1980s when that rite was increased to three times a week. In 1954, the centennial of our founding, Einsiedeln Abbey gave Saint Meinrad a replica of the statue that stands in the Abbey Church of Einsiedeln. A black Madonna, its regal beauty is often dressed in colored clothing to match the liturgical season. Even the stained glass window at the shrine represents St. Meinrad, in the 10th century, as having a devotion to her. Besides the community devotions, it has long been the practice for individuals to pray before her shrine, in particular, when the monks visited altars after compline.

One late afternoon, I was kneeling before Our Lady of Einsiedeln shrine when Fr. Francis came up and called me into the chapel area. He said: "Get me the missal." I brought it out for him. Then he said: "Open it to the Saturday Mass in honor of the Blessed Virgin." After I did that, he proceeded to recite the Introit, *Salve sancta parens*…"There, you see, I can read so I can offer Mass." The fact was, he was almost blind, and was reciting the passage by heart. He could no longer offer Mass. For a short time, the superiors took his name off the bulletin board where altars for offering Mass were assigned. Fr. Francis made such a fuss that finally they assigned him an altar so that the struggle would only be in the morning to prevent him from trying. Frequently during the day, he would grab a monk and ask him to show him which altar he was assigned to. With his name now back on the board, he was content, at least for the moment. Fr. Francis was also very devoted to the Divine Office. He insisted on being at Office. He sat behind the choir and insisted on having a book in hand. A junior monk was assigned to sit by him to provide him with a book. Sometimes for fun, they gave it to him upside down. He still held it religiously and proceeded to recite. He knew most of the psalms by heart. These are light moments that make us smile, but I think they also reveal how totally dedicated he was to Office and Mass. The attitude was ingrained in him. He was only one of many.

The rosary is a time-honored devotion to Mary. For many years, at least to about 1945, the rosary was recited daily in church as a community exercise. For many years, select phrases, according to the mystery of the decade being recited, were added to every Hail Mary after the words "thy Name, Jesus." (In the various editions of the *Novice Manual* the phrases were given in Latin, English and German, such as: Who rose again from the dead; Who ascended into heaven; Who did send the Holy Ghost; Who hast assumed thee into heaven; Who has crowned thee in heaven; etc.) Every monk is expected to have a personal rosary. Many recite it every day. It is still not unusual at all to see a monk carrying his rosary in prayer. Old Brother Philip carried it all the time. Bowed over as he was in his latter days, the rosary dragged on the ground. It was part of his environment. I remember one time in the dark of the church when Brother thought he was alone, he called out at our Lady Chapel, "*Wie Lang? Wie Lang?*" "How long before I can die?" was his plea. I remember being deeply touched by the sincerity and simplicity of his prayer.

The Angelus is another devotion that was a part of the Catholic culture. Many churches rang the bells for the Angelus three times a day. I suspect that at Saint Meinrad this custom was followed right from the earliest days. The Angelus bell still rings. The monks recite the prayer privately. For many years, though, it was recited publicly in choir after Lauds and the office closest to noon, None or Vespers during Lent.

Some of the major feasts were prepared for by novenas by the community. The prayers were said usually after dinner, during the visit to the Blessed Sacrament in church. Novenas in honor of Mary dotted the calendar. In more recent years, from around 1910 on, the Immaculate Conception (December 8) had a novena. Earlier, according to the 1889 *Novice Manual*, Christmas, the Feast of Assumption (August 15), and the Birth of Mary (September 8) had novenas as community exercises. That edition also provided for a private novena for our Sorrowful Mother in September. Novenas have not been a part of the community prayer life, probably since the 1960s.

Under the choir in the Abbey Church before the recent remodeling was a rather large space designated as the crypt. A huge grotto was built in the crypt honoring Our Lady of Lourdes. A kneeling statue of St. Bernadette of Soubirous was part of the shrine. There was a great devotion to Our Lady of Lourdes. Many monks and students prayed in that space every day. The stairs leading down into the crypt were of sandstone. I remember being impressed as a young student at how that stone had worn down from the many devotees who plied them. It was removed in a renovation in 1969.

A statue of our Blessed Mother has been on the grounds since the 1940s. Also, the very imposing seated Madonna in the niche over the doors of the church, I believe, was set in place in time for the centennial of the abbey in 1954. Mr. Jogerst had carved it from a solid block of Tennessee marble in the Abbey Art Shop. Getting it up into that niche was a great challenge. The piece weighed around 2,000 pounds. I was privileged to be able to watch the whole procedure. The model for his work was an early seal of the Abbey of Einsiedeln. Father Albert Kleber remarked to Mr. Jogerst that the shape of the image lacked modesty, which threw him into a rage. [Mr. Jogerst, a native of Germany, had been a prisoner of war in Kentucky. Fr. Peter Bremer invited him to come to work for the abbey after he was released from prison. Mr. Jogerst carved a number of other statues on campus and in the area. St. Benedict, St. Scholastica, St. Bede, and Christ the King were the others on our campus.]

A hill about a mile from the abbey has been named Monte Cassino. From very early days, there has been a shrine to our Lady there. A fine stone chapel, dedicated to Our Lady, was built and dedicated around 1870, and refurbished in 1940s. For many years, there was a procession from the Abbey Church to Monte Cassino on one of the rogation days. It was quite a sight to see the long winding procession of seminarians in their cassocks and surplices and the monks in their habits and cucullas making their way down the highway and up the hill. At the peak of our enrollment, close to 700 would be in that line. The rosary was recited as we walked, each group leading a separate recitation. Invariably, we would meet the parishioners from town coming down the hill as we were going up. There was a kind of cacophony as the two lines recited the rosary out of sync with each other. For years, too, Monte Cassino was a destination for a walk, a visit, and a return—a trip of a little more than an hour. Since the 1920s, the abbey has been responsible, usually through a few assigned monks, for devotions on the Sundays of May and October. *A Community Bulletin* note said that there were over 600 cars for each of the Sundays of October 2000, except one. These services consist of a short liturgy of the word, a devotional sermon, and the recitation of the rosary in procession around the top of the hill with a concluding blessing by the presiding monk. Some monks attend these services. They are not an official community activity, but it is one more indication of how the devotion to Our Blessed Mother is fostered in community members, and through them to the Catholics in the area surrounding the abbey.

In connection with Marian devotions, mention should be made of a phenomenon known as "Fatima Week." In the summer of 1948, a statue of Our Lady of Fatima was being carried from diocese to diocese throughout the country to foster devotion to Mary and to make more public her message at Fatima. Fr. Abbot Ignatius and a number of other monks wanted to make a "visit of the statue" a special occasion at Saint Meinrad, not only for those of us on the hill but also for the Catholic population in the parishes of southern Indiana. The abbey council affirmed his wish. There were 24 planning committees established, which ultimately involved a greater part of the community. For publicity, we had the help of a businessman in Evansville, Mr. W. Bussing, who directed a barrage of information all across southern Indiana. A complete description of all the activities has been published, which included most of the sermons and homilies preached during those days. [The Fatima Week Sermons. The complete text of the Sermons delivered on the occasion of the visit of the "Pilgrim Virgin" to St. Meinrad's Abbey, St. Meinrad, Indiana, August 14-20, 1948, with an Introduction, "The Story of Fatima Week in St. Meinrad" by the Right Reverend Ignatius Esser, O.S.B. Abbot of St. Meinrad's abbey. St. Meinrad, Indiana, A Grail Publication, 1949.]

Suffice it to say here that it became a major event in the history of the Abbey. The statue arrived in a motorcade, which was said to have been ten miles long. Fifteen state police officers were on hand to control the traffic. There were 749 automobiles in that motorcade. It was estimated that 125,000 people participated in one program or another over the course of the week. Each day there were 21 functions. There were communion Masses offered in the church every half hour from 6 a.m. to 11. The rosary was recited in church, along with a sermon, six times each day. A huge altar was erected on the grounds. A Pontifical High Mass was celebrated outside every day for the public. In sum, the whole occasion was one large statement of faith and devotion to Mary writ large on the Hill and in the minds and hearts of thousands of God's people. One priest of the Indianapolis Archdiocese wrote: "To my knowledge there has never been anything comparable to Fatima Week in the history of religion in the State of Indiana." Monsignor William C. McGrath, P.A., the person in charge of the touring statue said, in part, in his opening remarks: "During the past ten months, my dear friends, from Canada to the Gulf of Mexico, and through many dioceses and States of the Union, we have seen receptions accorded our Blessed Mother, but without wishing to indulge in a solitary word of pretense or flattery I will say that today's reception has been unsurpassed by anything we have seen in these United States."

To St. Benedict. Devotion to St. Benedict has always been fostered. The daily reading from the *Holy Rule*, the instructions of the novice masters, celebration of two major feasts in his honor, the novena before the March 21st feast, altar and statue in the church, shrine and statue in the crypt, as well as private prayers of intercession wove a pattern of devotion that permeated community life.

To St. Joseph. In a similar way, devotion to St. Joseph has always been in evidence. In the *Novice Manual* of 1889 there was a novena in his honor. It did not appear in later editions, but special prayers were attached to the other prayers normally said during the visit to the Blessed Sacrament after dinner during the month of March. An altar and statue were in the Abbey Church. A special shrine to St. Joseph was commissioned by Fr. Abbot Ignatius. Brother Herman carved the statue that still is enshrined in a sandstone nook in a lovely spot across the Anderson Valley. Its dedication was an occasion of great pomp. In more recent times, Fr. Abbot Lambert has fostered devotion to St. Joseph. He commissioned Fr. Donald to do a mural in the passage beneath the church and on the way to the crypt chapel, recently dedicated to St. Joseph.

Conclusion. This has been a romp through the practices of the monks of Saint Meinrad. No single devotion or custom would stand out as shaping the character of the monks, but I think the preponderance of little things adds up to a value-laden life that kept the monks focused in the "school of the Lord's service." Without doubt, more, similar practices could be brought up. It has been difficult for me to draw the line between the past and the present. It is evident that many of the small practices have been dropped. Certainly, the numerous lengthy novenas and verbal public prayers have been curtailed or dropped. Some died as the culture changed. Some were almost drastically uprooted. Some practices that were dropped have been picked up again. I am prepared to say that the next 150 years will see a somewhat similar pattern. I trust that the core values will continue to be preserved.

Homily for the Funeral of Sister Mary Charboneau, I.H.M.

Sr. Mary Charboneau was an important woman in my life. I met her when I was 13 years old in 1935. We became fast friends and remained so until her death in the mid-80s. I loved her with a tender affection and she responded in kind. I had preached for her 50 years of commitment and was ask by her to preside at her funeral.

Entrance Rite

In this Easter season, we celebrate with joy the passage of Jesus from death to life. We have gathered here tonight because our sister, Mary, has passed from life to death and we must consign her body to the grave. More is going on, though. Our sorrow at her passing and grief in this burial rite is made no less real when, at another level of faith, we celebrate her new life. She lives. With Jesus, she has passed now from death to life, and we celebrate with joy this other passage. Let us dispose ourselves for this double level of action. We need to grieve our loss. Our sister is gone, but we must also in faith celebrate her gain for she is alive and well with God.

Lord Jesus Christ, source of life and light, comfort us in our sorrow. Lord, have mercy.

Lord Jesus Christ, source of strength and courage, strengthen us in our weakness. Lord, have mercy.

Lord Jesus Christ, source of mercy and hope, forgive us our sins. Lord, have mercy.

Homily

The Gospel reading for the funeral Mass was from Luke 24:13-35.

You know Sister Mary chose this text we have just read from the Gospel of Luke. She made that choice in a season of long and cold nights of personal discomfort.

It fit hand in glove with the Gospel for the day she died. She could not have known. In any case, she chose well. If we take a few moments to reflect on this passage, we may not evoke the full meaning she intended, but I think we will be able to see its appropriateness for this occasion and come to appreciate at least some of the reasons she has asked to have it read tonight.

The encounter with Jesus on the road to Emmaus and what follows is surely one of the most charming and touching stories about Jesus, certainly of the resurrection stories. Here we see two disconsolate disciples trudging along the seven-mile road from Jerusalem to Emmaus. Disillusioned and disappointed, they hardly noted the stranger who joined them. They did not recognize him even when He opened the meaning of the Scripture to them. They invited Him to supper. It is likely that they were a married couple, Cleophas and his wife. At table in the breaking of the bread, they recognized Him. After He had gone, they recalled to each other how their hearts were on fire as He had expounded the scripture. So excited were they at the momentous realization, which they were now able to absorb, they rushed back the seven miles to Jerusalem to tell the others. There they heard of the other appearances of Jesus to the disciples and they told their exciting story of their encounter with Jesus along the road to Emmaus, and how He walked with them and shared a meal with them.

I believe Sister Mary would be partial to this story because she believed very deeply that Jesus is present in our encounters with one another. Sometimes He reveals Himself to us through the other; sometimes He reveals Himself to other through us. No encounter is insignificant. Often they are life-giving or life-healing moments in our otherwise deadening, humdrum lives. Many of us here will be forever grateful to Mary for being present to us in just such moments. Sharing this Scripture is her way of thanking us for our loving presence to her through the years and her way of urging us to be mindful of the presence of Jesus even in the seemingly insignificant encounters of our lives.

Perhaps more to the point, Sister Mary would have chosen this text because it foreshadows and reflects the reality of our liturgical assemblies and especially our Eucharistic liturgy. We all know how fully she entered into the meaning of our worship. She was a thanksgiving person. She focused all her energies toward making our worship authentic and responsible. Her musical contributions were not self-aggrandizing or even simply aesthetic interludes. She used her musical talent to enhance the celebration, to provide responses to readings and to nurture the faith experience taking place. The disciples on the road had the Scripture laid open before them and they shared bread with Jesus at table. We in our Mass have both the Liturgy of the Word and the liturgy of the Eucharist, which is completed in the sharing of His Body and Blood from the table of the Lord. I think this is a further and more cogent reason for Mary's choosing this text for us tonight.

This one last time she speaks to us. This one last time she teaches us to strive to deepen our appreciation for word and sacrament. She teaches us to find in these things, as she did, an encounter with the living God.

It is difficult to let go. There are so many things—even very personal things—each of us might like to say at this time. My own fond memories of Mary go back 50 years, even into this chapel. Not too many months ago, there were rounds of celebrations for Mary's 50 years of service to the Lord and His church. At that time, she was overwhelmed by the many signs of love, respect and appreciation that were heaped on her from every side. How grateful we can all be that we took the time to do the things we did. The consolation of those hours helped her face the soul-shaking weeks and months just past. She bore them in peace, looking forward with joy to a new life with Jesus, regretting only that she must leave us behind for a time. She passed through that narrow gate now, and who can even imagine what our loving Savior has had in store for her. We will miss her, but we must believe that she is with her God.

For our part, we can do no better, here in this sacred space where she labored for most of her life, we can do no better, than to encounter Jesus in word and sacrament in the sharing of these Scriptures and the breaking of the bread. And then, perhaps, we too will be able to say, as did the couple on the road to Emmaus: "Were not our hearts aglow as we did these things!"

May she rest in peace.

Another Arrangement by Titles

Personal Stories

Family Stories

Community Stories

Homilies and Spiritual Topics

Miscellaneous Stories

978-0-595-35455-9
0-595-35455-6

Made in the USA
Lexington, KY
06 November 2011